THE
EARLY
PIANO

THE EARLY PIANO

C. F. COLT

with

Antony Miall

STAINER & BELL: LONDON

First published in 1981
by Stainer & Bell Limited
82 High Road London N2 9PW

Typeset by Pierson LeVesley Ltd
Printed in Great Britain by Sackville Press Billericay Ltd

Produced by Editorial and Production Services Ltd London

ISBN 0 85249 572 2

CONTENTS

PREFACE

This book is the outcome of many years' research and thought. It is not meant to be a complete guide to the history or repair of historical keyboard instruments. On such a large subject one can only hint at the broad lines of approach. It is not even an instruction book on how to play the fortepiano. Nearly a hundred various and related types of 'piano' have been selected for description from my somewhat cumbersome collection of historical keyboard instruments, with a view to tracing the history and development of the Early Piano. Many people have asked me to write up the Collection 'in toto'. This would be a boring job – for readers as well as the writer – because so many instruments are either duplicates or differ from 'twin sister' models by only the slightest and very often unimportant details, and when one realises that I have had at times nearly as many as 150 keyboard instruments, it would be a major undertaking.

Only a few years ago buying an early piano, unless it had been converted into a writing desk or dressing-table, would have been thought an act of lunacy.

Perhaps the turning point came just before the war when Mozart's own grand piano was restored most painstakingly in 1936 by Dr Rück in Nuremberg. This piano is now housed at Mozart's birthplace in Getreidegasse in Salzburg in perfect playing order. This achievement, which has been documented in a small book, *Mozart Gedenkstätten in Salzburg der Internationalen Stiftung Mozarteum; und Köchel Verzeichnis*, was a revelation to those sceptics who thought an early piano was a poor sort of harpsichord.

Since then people are at last appreciating the sound of a properly restored early piano. Records have been made using such instruments for which the music was originally composed, and a number of ensembles, here and abroad, are using only old instruments, or at least faithful copies, so that the sound of the music is authentic.

In 1956 I was flattered to be asked by Benjamin Britten if I would lend my Mozart-type piano for the final concert at Broadcasting House celebrating the 200th anniversary of Mozart's birth. This live concert was one of the first of such to be broadcast in England. It was a great success and the demand for early pianos for such music started.

Many people want to own an early piano, but when they do find one have no idea of its date, since many makers only numbered their pianos. I am sure this book will help them in their search.

C.F. COLT
Thierachern

LES TROIS SOEURS

RONDINOS

pour le PIANO à 6 mains

'The Three Sisters' playing a Streicher fortepiano appear on the cover of a collection of rondinos arranged for six hands by Czerny. The three girls also grace an English edition published by Cocks in London, but with different dress and hair-dos reflecting the English fashions of the time.

THE HISTORY

At the beginning of the eighteenth century fashionable music in Europe leant far more towards the homophonic than the contrapuntal. Even the great J.S.Bach's sons referred to their father as 'Old Wig' and made sport of his rather old-fashioned style of composition and his predilection for the harpsichord and clavichord. He, in his turn, considered the early piano as being only 'fit for rondos'. And there can be no doubt that the first Silbermann instruments of this type he encountered were not to his liking.

However, with the new trends in music, the harpsichord was fast becoming unsuitable – unable to give sufficient shape and dynamic line to the melodies that were emerging as focal points in the new compositions. Certainly the clavichord was capable of graduated dynamic variation, but its volume was inadequate for anything other than the most intimate gatherings.

The stage was definitely set for the appearance of a new instrument – one which combined the volume of the harpsichord with the expressiveness of the clavichord. It is small wonder, then, that Scipione Maffei was so enthusiastic in his *Giornale dei letterati d'Italia* (1711):

> It is known to everyone who delights in music, that one of the principal means by which the skilful in that art derive the secret of especially delighting those who listen, is the piano and forte in the theme and its response, or in the gradual diminution of tone little by little, and then returning suddenly to the full power of the instrument; which artifice is frequently used and with marvellous effect, in the great concerts of Rome . . .
>
> Now, of this diversity and alteration of tone, in which instruments played with the bow especially excel, the harpsichord is entirely deprived, and it would have been thought a vain endeavour to propose to make it so that it should participate in this power. Nevertheless, so bold an invention has been no less happily conceived than executed in Florence, by Signor Bartolomeo Cristofali [Cristofori], of Padua, harpsichord-player of the most serene Prince of Tuscany . . .
>
> He has already made three, of the usual size of other harpsichords, and they have all succeeded to perfection. The production of greater or less sound depends on the degree of power with which the player presses on the keys, by regulating which not only the piano and forte are heard, but also the gradations and diversity of power, as in a violoncello . . . This is properly a chamber instrument,

and is not intended for church music, nor for a great orchestra . . . It is certain that to accompany a singer, and to play with one other instrument, or even for a moderate concert, it succeeds perfectly: although this is not its principal intention, but rather to be played alone, like the lute, harp, viols of six strings, and other most sweet instruments. But really the great cause of the opposition which this new instrument has encountered is, in general, the want of knowledge how, at first, to play it; because it is not sufficient to know how to play perfectly upon instruments with the ordinary finger board but, being a new instrument, it requires a person who, understanding its capabilities, shall have made a particular study of its effects, so as to regulate the measure of force required on the keys and the effects of decreasing it, also to choose pieces suited to it for delicacy, and especially for the movement of the parts, that the subject may be heard distinctly in each . . .

Maffei's enthusiasm was certainly not misplaced. Very few of Cristofori's instruments survive today. Two of them are dated 1720 and 1726. Both are remarkable and many of their constructional principles survived for over one hundred years, until the pianoforte had become arguably the most important musical instrument in the Western world.

As Maffei states, Cristofori was employed by Prince Ferdinand dei Medici as harpsichord player and harpsichord maker and it is, therefore, hardly surprising that his new instrument not only looked exactly like a harpsichord but was also christened 'gravicembalo col piano e forte' – a harpsichord with soft and loud. But there the similarity ends. The later of the two surviving instruments, now restored, is in Leipzig, and recordings of it betray no trace of harpsichord timbre. The sound is unmistakably that of an early piano.

History is full of prophets without honour in their own countries and Bartolomeo Cristofori swells their ranks. He died in 1731 with the sound of harpsichords ringing in his ears. Italy was unimpressed by the new instrument. It was unsuitable for the performance of opera – so much in vogue in the early eighteenth century – and chamber music was more at home in colder climates where people spent so many more hours indoors.

But dissatisfaction with the limitations of the harpsichord and clavichord was not the sole prerogative of the Prince of Tuscany's harpsichord maker. Throughout Western Europe musicians were beginning to look for an alternative instrument which would give them the flexibility of dynamic and the 'singing' quality that they longed for. North of the Alps, however, lovers of music found their inspiration in the sounds produced by a German who made his fortune as a travelling entertainer.

Pantaleon Hebenstreit was born in Eisleben in 1667 and started his professional life as a dancing master and violinist in Leipzig. By the time he was thirty, however, he had made himself an enormous reputation as a performer on the dulcimer. This instrument he had greatly enlarged, making it four times its original size, with 180 strings. His performances in Paris in 1705 caused a furore, and Louis XIV suggested that the new instrument should be called a 'Pantaleon' after its great exponent. The name was adopted and Hebenstreit went from strength to strength, being appointed 'pantaleonist' at the court of Dresden in 1714. Here he was heard by Kuhnau who observed that the pantaleon was superior to the fashionable harpsichord in that it was capable of producing a graduated dynamic. Gottlieb Schröter, a teacher of keyboard playing, also heard Hebenstreit and immediately devised two actions – one-upstriking and the other down-striking – for playing the harpsichord with hammers. Financial support, however, was not forthcoming, and Schröter's project had to be abandoned. Thus for a second time the emergent instrument was rejected and the stage was once again set for the appearance of a new 'inventor'.

The Court Poet at Dresden, König, published in 1725 a translation of Maffei's article on Cristofori's *gravicembalo*, and within a year his friend the clavichord maker, Gottfried Silbermann, had produced two similar instruments. It seems almost superfluous to note that neither of these pianofortes found favour and that Gottfried Silbermann died in 1753 in relative obscurity. One can't help wondering if any musical instrument ever had so lengthy or troublesome a gestation.

It was one of Silbermann's apprentices who eventually untied the Gordian knot. Christian Ernst Friederici, continuing with his master's experiments, eventually produced a small 'square' piano based on the design of the clavichord which, with characteristic German humour, he called a '*fortbien*'. Friederici's *fortbiens* had an enormous success, being, according to one authority, 'famed and scattered over half the world'. At last a rudimentary piano had found acceptance and the way ahead was clear for its development and improvement.

The Seven Years War in Germany resulted in 1760 in twelve instrument makers arriving in England. Among these 'twelve apostles', as they became known, were several of Silbermann's apprentices, including Johann Christoph Zumpe. Zumpe built up an extremely successful business concentrating almost entirely on 'square' pianos for which his name became virtually a synonym in the second half of the eighteenth century.

11

These instruments, selling at from £20, became as ubiquitous as Friederici's had been and there can be no doubt that they were very satisfactory. In 1768 J.C.Bach gave the first ever piano recital on one of Zumpe's instruments at the Thatched House in London. The particular instrument had cost him £50; apparently it was considered a bargain by both the performer and the audience. The evening and the piano were hailed as successes, and demand for 'Zumpes' grew apace until, according to Burney, there was scarcely a house in the kingdom where there wasn't one. They were even exported and the *'piano anglais'*, as it became known on the continent, caused a furore.

The next thirty years saw an ever increasing acceptance of the new instrument. Burney's own nephew was appointed 'to the pianoforte' at Drury Lane in 1770, and in 1773 the first real pianoforte music was published – Muzio Clementi's 3 Sonatas (op. 2). Finally that most conservative of all musical institutions – the King's Band – replaced its harpsichord with a pianoforte in 1795.

But the pianos used by J.C. Bach in 1768 and in the previous year by Dibdin to accompany Miss Brickler at Covent Garden, by no means standardised instruments, were very closely related to the harpsichord and clavichord. The complete acceptance of the piano was a gradual process and the demand for harpsichords was still sizeable.

Nevertheless instrument makers both in England and on the Continent continued to experiment and by the 1780s two distinct types of piano had emerged – the Viennese (strictly German) and the English. The Viennese piano was lighter in construction than its English counterpart, usually bi-chord throughout and with lighter leather-covered hammers. Its delicate tone contrasted with the more sonorous trichord timbre of the English piano, whose more complicated action and less efficient damping made for a heavier instrument altogether. Whereas the English piano demanded further development, the Viennese product of a maker like Johann Andreas Stein was perfect enough for Mozart, who wrote to his father in 1777: 'This time I shall begin at once with Stein's pianofortes. Before I had seen any of his make, Späth's claviers had always been my favourites. But now I much prefer Stein's.'

While Mozart was rhapsodising over Stein's pianos in Augsburg, John Broadwood in England had been apprenticed to the harpsichord maker, Shudi; had married Shudi's daughter; had become a partner in his father-in-law's firm and had started to devote his time almost entirely to the development of the pianoforte. By 1783 he had patented his design for a vastly improved square piano with efficient underdampers. Thereafter he turned his attention to the grand pianoforte, producing by 1788 an instrument of far greater sonority than its predecessors with greater evenness of tone throughout its range and remarkable dynamic flexibility.

Shudi's son, who had been Broadwood's partner since 1773, finally retired in 1793, and it is significant that Broadwood produced no more harpsichords after that date, concentrating his energies entirely in the direction of the expanding piano market. During the next ten years he produced some 400 instruments a year – 300 square pianos and 100 grands. Such an output contrasts sharply with the average number of instruments produced in one year by an eighteenth-century harpsichord maker who expected to complete a modest twenty. The demand for pianos was growing apace.

The French Revolution brought further foreign makers to England, the most important of whom was Sebastien Erard. Erard set up his factory in Great Marlborough Street in 1792 at a time when London was fast becoming the piano-manufacturing capital of the world. The beginnings of the steady growth of middle-class affluence which was to characterise the Victorian period provided an ever-increasing market, and makers developed and improved designs until in the middle of the nineteenth century they had produced an instrument which was virtually a modern piano. The early nineteenth century saw more upright grand pianos, the rise of the cottage piano and pianino, the patenting by Erard in 1821 of his double escapement – a refinement of the action which allowed easier repetition of notes – as well as a host of what can only be called gimmicks like this one advertised in *Musical Times*:

> There is very shortly to be brought before the public a new kind of pianoforte, the novelty of which consists in its having a second row of hammers, that being worked by means of a pedal, in the ordinary way, produce the sound of an octave upon the striking of a single note, and of a double octave if the two notes are struck. The instrument is about the size of an ordinary piano . . .

Hand in hand with this phenomenal development of the piano came a vastly expanded general interest in music. Just as the piano became a status symbol in Victorian homes, blending its beautifully decorated case into its opulent surroundings, so the appreciation of music – albeit not always very good music – became the hallmark of gentility to the middle classes.

England became a very attractive concert platform for visiting foreign musicians, and foremost among these musicians were the virtuoso pianists, who were welcomed with rapturous appreciation.

Steibelt, Cramer, Hummel and Dussek all played new Broadwood pianos in London, the latter turning the piano at right angles to the audience so that his magnificent profile could be admired. Sigismond Thalberg earned an incredible £24,000 from his concert appearances in 1840, half of these, at least, having been given in England.

Chopin played to the music-hungry English. According to his memoirs they found his playing 'like water'. He observed, rather ungallantly, that English lady pianists played the wrong notes with 'such feeling'. Mendelssohn's successes here, both as a pianist and a composer are part of musical history. But it was, perhaps, for the salon lion – Franz Liszt – that the most enraptured paeans were kept:

The Abbé himself seemed to fall into a dream; his fingers fell again lightly on the keys . . . Then rose from the bass the song of the Angelus, or rather, it seemed like the vague emotion of one who, as he passes, hears in the ruins of some wayside cloister the ghosts of old monks humming their drowsy melodies, as the sun goes down rapidly, and the purple shadows of Italy steal over the land, out of the orange west!

We sat motionless . . . Liszt was almost as motionless: his fingers seemed quite independent, chance ministers of his soul. The dream was broken by a pause; then came back the little swaying passage of bells, tossing high up in the evening air, the half-bar of silence, the broken rhythm – and the Angelus was rung . . .

It is useless for me to attempt a description of a performance every phrase of which will be implanted in my memory, and on my heart as long as I live . . .the magic notes falling like a soft shower of pearls or liquid drops from a fountain – blown spray falling hither and thither, and changing into rainbow tints in its passage, as the harmonic progression kept changing and tossing the fugitive fragments of melody . . . I drew my chair gently nearer, I almost held my breath, not to miss a note. There was a strange concentrated anticipation about Liszt's playing unlike anything I have ever heard – not for a moment could the ear cease listening; each note seemed prophetic of the next, each yielded in importance to the next; one felt that in the soul of the player the whole piece existed from the beginning – as one and indivisible, like a poem in the heart of a poet. The playing of the bars had to be gone through seriatim; but there were glimpses of a higher state of intuition, in which one could read thoughts without words, and possess the soul of music, without the intervention of bars and keys and strings; all the mere elements seemed to fade, nothing but perception remained.

My Musical Life, H.R.Haweis 1875

It is hardly surprising that piano-makers welcomed and encouraged this proliferation of piano recitals. The temptation for members of the audience to buy a piano and to try and do likewise must have been overwhelming.

The Great Exhibition of 1851 naturally reflected the enthusiasm of the day: 178 pianos were exhibited by no fewer than 102 different manufacturers. Many of the instruments were beautiful pieces of furniture like the Schneider Grand Piano illustrated on page 127. Such pianos were certainly not cheap, and in 1851 even a modest square piano cost between sixty and seventy guineas – roughly the equivalent to a year's wages for a clerk or schoolmaster. By the end of the century, however, the price of a cottage upright piano had fallen to £25, which represented only three months salary for a man in the same profession. Annual production figures in England had risen to a staggering 500,000, and it must have been rare to find a house in the land that could not boast an instrument.

As early as the 1860s it had been possible to buy a piano by hire purchase – known as the 'Three Year System'. This brought it well within the financial grasp even of a Yorkshire miner:

> Fifteen years ago it was scarcely possible to find a collier who could write his name and now every child he has can read and write. A great number own their own houses as freeholders, and the system is on the increase. Some of them have pianos and harmoniums, and even perambulators.
>
> *Musical Times*, August 1873

An interesting glimpse of Victorian priorities!

It is hard for us today to understand the piano mania of the last century. In an age when the motor car has become the primary status symbol, pianos in the home are almost as rare as aspidistras. The upheavals of two World Wars, the inventions of the gramophone, the radio and the television have all contributed to the decline in 'home entertainment' of which the piano was the mighty corner-stone. Nowadays it is possible to hear great symphonies at the flick of a switch. For our ancestors it was a question of turning to what one Victorian writer called 'the orchestra of the home' and a score in piano reduction. Our houses are smaller and most of us could not accommodate a grand piano even if we wanted one. But in the century of mass production it is very comforting to look back to a time when craftsmen were concerned to make something practical appear beautiful at the same time, and the fact that so many early pianos are still both prompts one to wonder how many of our status symbols will perform as well and look as well when they are over two hundred years old.

1. HEILMAN GRAND (*c.*1775)

This fortepiano is the earliest 'grand' in the Collection: it is also one of the best. It has been recorded a number of times and is typical of the kind of instrument used by C.P.E.Bach, J.C.Bach and Mozart. Indeed, to hear the music of these composers played on this Heilman is a revelation. The tone is authentic and the music sounds as it really must have done when it was first composed and played.

Though not dated, this piano has all the features of a very early Heilman. It is numbered 194, and while it is not known exactly how Heilman numbered his pianos, we may fairly assume that he would have followed the example of his contemporaries, who often started numbering their pianos at 100 to give the impression that they had made more pianos than they actually had.

Matthäus Heilman was born on 10 May 1744 in Hofheim, Taunus, near Frankfurt, but set up business in Mainz. In 1777 he married one Appolonia Müller, was made a freeman of the City of Mainz, and was taken into the Goldsmiths' Guild. On 2 April 1788 he was appointed tuner to the court at an annual salary of one hundred florins. Besides tuning the court instruments, he was expected to keep them all in a good state of repair. Conflicting authorities give his date of death as 1798 or 1817. His son, Joseph Heilman, also had a reputation as an excellent piano maker, but he seems to have returned to Frankfurt to build up his connections there.

Newly-discovered correspondence between Heilman senior and a local dignitary in Mainz sheds an amusing light on the rivalry and professional jealousy that existed between these early piano makers. In reply to an earnest enquiry, Heilman manages to supply all the information required while at the same time splendidly putting his contemporary, Stein, in his place:

> You want to buy from me a piano-forte like Stein's, whose pianos I know only too well as I have already earned much money by repairing them. I should be sorry if my instruments should need such frequent repair.
>
> At the moment I have nothing finished here but two piano-fortes in walnut, the best of which you can pick out. Their price, which includes packing and delivery from here by river, would not be higher than 18 carolins. But the same piano in mahogany with brass mouldings would be about 24 carolins. These have to be ordered in advance, but can be delivered in ten weeks.
>
> I also make small piano-fortes – 5ft 5 ins long and 2ft 9 ins wide – which for their size are quite

HEILMAN GRAND

Length: 84"   *Width:* 37½"   *Depth of case:* 9½"   *Height:* 27½" (floor to keyboard)
Pedals: Genouillères (knee levers)   *Case:* Walnut   *Legs:* Square tapered   *Keyboard:* Ebony naturals/bone-covered beech accidentals
Compass: Five octaves *F,–f'''*   *Octave size:* 6⅛"   *Strings:* Replaced   *Wrest pins:* Original, but reduced in size above *e''*.
Damping: Wedge-shaped leather-covered to *c''*, thick buff leather above   *Bridge:* Continuous
Action: Viennese   *Hammer coverings:* Buff leather   *Recorded:* Decca

effective. The price of these in oak is 13 carolins and in mahogany, 18 carolins. However, in a large room the larger piano is better. The undersides of the lids are painted.

It will not be necessary for me to go into the quality of these instruments as my products speak for themselves. You yourself will have heard them praised and references to them from near and far, wherever they have been sent, must have reached all ears. . . .

I remain etc.,

Matthäus Heilman 1787

Hermann von Helmholtz, the celebrated physicist and Doctor of Acoustics, was at one time the owner of the Heilman grand no. 194.

Haxby square of 1774. This might be Haxby's first square. It is to all intents and purposes like Zumpes of the same period, with 'short' compass.

2. GANER SQUARE (1779)

The small 'piano-forte' referred to by Matthäus Heilman (see p. 18) was undoubtedly a square piano, as its width would give too short a compass for a grand as late as 1787.

Makers were never particular in their terminology in referring to their pianos. All Christopher Ganer's 'squares' are called 'fortepiano' in the 1770s; Heilman's 'grand' of 1775 was also called 'fortepiano', though by his letter of 1787 he writes of his 'piano-fortes'. Spanish owners in 1780 refer to their 'fuerte-pianos'; in France, an Erard of 1818 (see p. 67) was still called 'fortepiano'; in Vienna, Graf used 'forte-piano' between 1830 and 1840, Streicher in 1853; and the instrument is *still* called 'fortepiano' in Russia and Yugoslavia today.

But in music publications and concert programmes printed between 1775 and 1850, 'pianoforte' and 'fortepiano' seem to have been interchangeable. Nowadays we use 'fortepiano' as a term of convenience preferable to 'antique piano', 'historical piano' or even 'early piano'.

Ganer's square pianos were always very elegant – perhaps more so than most of those made by others amongst the 'twelve apostles' – the twelve piano makers who left Germany in about 1760 to avoid political oppression as well as to make a better living in London or Paris (see p. 11).

The design of square pianos seems to have changed little between 1760 and 1785. They apparently fulfilled the needs and desires of both composers and players of the time. Their actions were simple – so simple as to be foolproof. The tone and volume were sufficient for smallish rooms and, as yet, not much 'pianistic' music was being written.

This instrument has five octaves, and has three handstops boxed in on the left-hand side of the instrument. The first stop is a buff, which presses a thin strip of 'buff' leather onto the underside of the strings to give a pizzicato effect (as if plucked in a harpsichord), and the other two activate a divided damper-raiser – one on the lower half of the keyboard and the other on the higher. This sort of damper-raiser cannot have been very practical, as it means removing the hand from the keyboard in order to activate it.

Another square piano by the same maker, also in the Collection (dated *c.*1795) shows a very early use of what might be termed an *agraffe*. This is a lead strip over which the strings pass in front of the nut before the guide pins, giving an increased clarity to the sound.

GANER SQUARE

Length: 19½″   *Width:* 59¾″   *Depth of case:* 7¾″   *Height:* 28½″ (floor to keyboard)
Case: Mahogany crossbanded in satinwood   *Legs:* Square tapered   *Keyboard:* Ivory naturals/ebony accidentals
Compass: Five octaves   *Octave size:* 6¼″   *Strings:* Partly original   *Wrest pins:* Original   *Damping:* Mopstick
Bridge: Continuous   *Action:* English single   *Hammer coverings:* Buff leather

3. HANCOCK GRAND (1775-1780)

An advertisement in the first edition of *The Observer* dated 4 December 1791 announces:

> John Crang Hancock – patentee of the grand and small pianoforte with spring key touch, harp and flute stops, most respectfully informs amateurs and professors that he has invented and brought to perfection, violins, tenors and violoncellos (for which a patent is soliciting) so capital in tone, as to be pronounced, by all who have heard them, greatly superior to the productions of those celebrated makers Stainer, Amati, Stradivarius &c.,&c.
>
> Of these instruments a few only are as yet finished; therefore they are not at present offered for sale, but merely as specimens, for the inspection and trial of cognoscenti and masters, to whose sole use Hancock has appropriated the first floor of his house in Parliament Street.
>
> N.B. The Ladies are respectfully informed, that a most capital collection of patent grand and portable pianofortes possessing unequalled brilliancy and sweetness of tone, are on sale as above, price from twenty to eighty guineas each.

It is doubtful that 'the Ladies' would have found an instrument like this one in Mr Hancock's showrooms. Shaped like a spinet with a curiously old-fashioned walnut veneer, it seems likely to have been made as a special order for someone who either wanted it to look like an earlier instrument, or wished his piano to marry up with furniture of an earlier date. The tone of the piano is, however, absolutely reminiscent of a grand piano and the volume is comparable to that of the 'large' piano by Broadwood dated 1787 (see p. 41). Another curious feature of the design is that the long side of the instrument is carefully veneered; this suggests that it was intended to be seen, and not pushed against a wall as most keyboard instruments like the harpsichord were (this accounts for so many harpsichords having no 'finish' on their long sides).

Internally the layout is just like that of a spinet, but the action is somewhat complicated. It cannot be slid out of the case for adjustment. Instead the piano has to be taken off its stand and turned on its back, and four screws undone to release the mechanism.

A similar arrangement is found in the larger grand piano, also almost certainly by Hancock, illustrated on page 25, but in that one there is only a butterfly hook to be undone instead of the four screws. The action is hinged on the left-hand side and can be then attended to quite easily. One fascinating point about this larger grand piano is that it has an obviously false nameboard which, to go by the wording, must be post-1807. The piano itself is much earlier – between 1775 and 1781. The

HANCOCK GRAND

Length: 71″   *Width:* Spinet-shaped   *Depth of case:* 9″   *Height:* 27¾″ (floor to keyboard)
Pedals: One sustaining   *Case:* Walnut   *Legs:* Trestle stand – turned baluster legs
Keyboard: Ivory naturals/ebony accidentals   *Compass:* Five octaves less *F*, sharp   *Octave size:* 6½″   *Strings:* Replaced
Wrest pins: Replaced   *Damping:* Hancock's own patent   *Bridge:* Continuous
Action: Hancock's own patent (see *The Pianoforte* by R.E.M.Harding)   *Hammer coverings:* Buff leather

keyboard surround is in dark wood – perhaps a burr walnut or some sort of 'diseased' hardwood. The layout is similar to a harpsichord's and the compass is a short five octaves. The instrument is supported on a trestle stand, and has one pedal to lift the dampers and a knee-stop to move the action to the left. There is one continuous bridge. In spite of the fake nameboard, there is no doubt that the instrument is old, and a possible theory for the existence of the spurious attribution is that someone faked the nameboard so that the piano would appear more modern than it in fact was, perhaps after a major repair and overhaul in about 1808.

The legs and casework are elaborate for a date of *c.*1800; tapered, inlaid legs with castors, very expensive mahogany veneer on the sides, and elaborate inlays and crossbanding with green stained rosettes in the corners of the panels. This must be one of the earliest existing English grand pianos.

Little is known of the life of John Crang Hancock, who is better known as a harpsichord maker than for his pianos. It is, however, pleasing to note that a descendant of his is writing a history of Hancock's life and work.

In 1853 the firm of Streicher was still using the word 'fortepiano' for its medal-winning instruments.

This very elaborately inlaid piano would appear to be by Crang Hancock, *c.* 1780.

'Invention' of the pianoforte is generally credited to Bartolomeo Cristofori, working at the very beginning of the eighteenth century. Like all early piano manufacturers, Cristofori was originally a harpsichord maker, and early pianos are often almost indistinguishable from the instruments from which they were developed. As we have seen, Hancock in England was primarily a harpsichord maker.

Jakob Kirckman was born in 1710 near Strasbourg, in the small town of Bischweiler which was then part of Germany. He emigrated to London and found employment with a Flemish harpsichord maker, Tabel, who had come from the Ruckers School and had found his own way to London in about 1680. When his master died, Kirckman married his widow and inherited the whole business, lock, stock and barrel. Dr Burney relates that the whole manoeuvre took Kirckman a very short time. Just one month after Tabel's death, his young apprentice proposed to the widow at breakfast-time, and they were married before noon!

In 1742 Kirckman moved his business to Great Pulteney Street in the immediate neighbourhood of his former fellow-apprentice Shudi. The friendly rivalry which had meanwhile developed between the two men stimulated both to the highest peak of perfection, and helped to make the English harpsichord of the period the *ne plus ultra* of that instrument. Fanny Burney described Kirckman as 'the first harpsichord maker of the times', and Forkel's *Musical Almanack for Germany for 1782* described his instruments as 'uncommonly well built'. Referring to their beautiful tone the same publication observes also that 'for them 400–600 Rhenian Thalers are paid'. Dated 1781, Kirckman's harpsichord is unique in having a set of four drawers set into its stand. Although it was common later for square pianos to have drawers, harpsichord makers did not, as a rule, go in for them . . . but Kirckman was also a maker of pianos.

The beautifully figured case has brass strap hinges to the lid and the legs of the stand are, curiously, of stained beech, suggesting that the stand and drawers were made by a small 'outside' joiner who lacked large scantlings of mahogany. The keyboard surround is of burr walnut, showing that walnut was still being used for decorative purposes in England in 1781.

There are two eight-foot registers and one four-foot, and the plectra are made of a plastic substitute for quill — necessary nowadays when the supply of fresh quills is not what it was in the eighteenth century. This plastic material is easy to work with, but cannot compare with crow or raven quill which produces a much smoother and less scratchy tone. Of the four hand stops those on the

KIRCKMAN HARPSICHORD

Length: 86½″   *Width:* 36⅛″   *Depth of case:* 11¾″   *Height:* 26½″ (floor to keyboard)
Pedals: One – machine stop   *Case:* Mahogany   *Legs:* Trestle stand – square Chippendale legs
Keyboard: Ivory and ebony   *Compass:* Five octaves less *F*, sharp   *Octave size:* 6⅜″   *Strings:* Replaced
Wrest pins: Original   *Bridge:* Continuous   *Action:* Harpsichord

left-hand side bring in one set of eight-foot strings and a buff stop, and those on the right-hand side control the four-foot and second set of eight-foot strings. The single pedal, when depressed, removes first one set of eight-foot strings and then the four-foot set. When released, it produces the full harpsichord 'grand jeu'. The compass of the keyboard is the usual English 'short' five octaves, lacking F,.

Jakob Kirckman died advanced in years leaving a staggering £200,000 – a testament to the success of his business as well as to his shrewd investment. His marriage to Tabel's widow was childless, and the firm passed to his nephew Abraham Kirckman who had been a partner since 1773. It was Abraham's son Joseph who paid especial attention to the manufacture of pianofortes. He was succeeded by his sons Joseph (1790-1877) and Henry John (died c.1873). When the firm eventually closed down in 1896, the last owner again bore the name of Joseph.

Späth and Schmahl portable piano. Mozart is reputed to have had one by this maker.

'Workbox' pianos and similar curios had become popular by the early nineteenth century, but they have little in common with this instrument (numbered 62) which was obviously designed as a serious piano.

Although it is small – just four octaves in compass, the tone of this instrument is full and much less muted than a clavichord's. There are no handstops or pedals. Unusually the wrest pins are placed in the front of the instrument and not on the right-hand side. This arrangement is supposed to have been a Broadwood patent of 1784, although Shudi and Broadwood did produce a 'square' in 1780 using the new layout – presumably a prototype.

The satinwood case is crossbanded in rosewood, and instead of legs there are four soft leather pads to protect the surface on which the piano is put. As a finishing touch there is even a tiny folding music rest which packs away easily when the instrument is closed.

Small German portable piano by Mahr of Wiesbaden, *c.* 1804, now in the Deutsches Museum, Munich.

VEREL PORTABLE

Length: 38″ *Width:* 13″ *Depth of case:* 5¾″
Case: Satinwood crossbanded in rosewood *Keyboard:* Ivory naturals/ebony accidentals
Compass: Four octaves less *F* sharp *Octave size:* 6⅛″ *Strings:* Replaced *Wrest pins:* Original *Damping:* Mopstick
Bridge: Continuous *Action:* English single *Hammer coverings:* Buff leather

6. MERLIN CLAVIORGANUM (1784)

Another curiosity of these early years, this instrument, which at first sight looks like a rather heavy square piano, turns out on closer inspection to be two instruments in one. It is both piano and organ, designed by an inventor of great ingenuity.

John Joseph Merlin was born at Huys near Namur in Belgium on 17 September 1735, and died in London in 1804. He had settled in Paris by the time he was nineteen but made his permanent home in London from 1760. Here he became companion to the Spanish Ambassador. As an inventor he is probably better known to most people for his 'Bath' or invalid chair propelled by the occupant's own hands, and for his rollerskates. He also combined a piano and harpsichord as early as 1780, and produced a 'downstriking' grand in 1786, far earlier than any other maker. Merlin's quadro-chord stringing also antedated Graf's by nearly forty years.

Because of the extra weight of the claviorganum, the maker found it necessary to support the case on four sturdy legs and six castors – one on each leg and one in the middle of each stretcher. The case is prettily decorated with satinwood crossbanding. The music rest is of the long organ-type, suitable for 'landscapewise' organ music. At each side of the rest is a small flap designed to take a candlestick.

The piano part of the instrument is intriguing in itself. Superficially it looks like any other square piano of the period, with the usual five octaves and the wrest pins on the right. But the damper mechanism is based on the mopstick principle – so cleverly designed that it can be removed in one unit, and put back in a matter of seconds, merely by undoing a couple of metal butterfly catches. This makes for easy repair and adjustment. There is a handstop which disengages the hammer mechanism by propping the hammers up just under the strings. A further handstop pulls the action forward a fraction of an inch, allowing the hammers to strike only one of the two strings. Since the hammers are in a straight line this comparatively simple 'una corda' device works well. On most other square pianos the layout is such that the hammers are set on a slight curve, so that this method would not work.

The organ part of the instrument consists of a single stop of wooden pipes at eight-foot pitch. The lowest pipe – $F_{,}$ – is signed 'R & W Gray 31st January 1784'. W.L.Sumner in his book *The Organ* writes that Robert Gray established a factory in London in 1774, in which he was succeeded by William Gray and then by John Gray. It is possible that Robert and William Gray only supplied the pipes for this claviorganum, but it seems more likely that they built the whole organ for Merlin. The date also suggests that both organ and piano were built at the same time and that the organ was not a later addition to an already existing square piano.

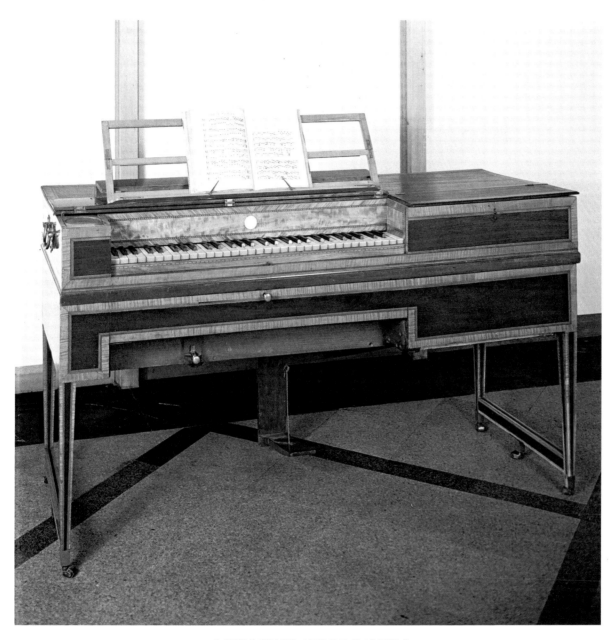

MERLIN CLAVIORGANUM

Length: 59½″   *Width:* 23½″   *Depth of case:* 7½″   *Height:* 30½″ (floor to keyboard)
Pedals: Two – handstop sustaining/pump pedal   *Case:* Mahogany crossbanded in satinwood   *Legs:* Square tapered
Keyboard: Ivory naturals/ebony accidentals   *Compass:* Five octaves $F,-f'''$ *Octave size:* 6⅞″
Strings: Restrung in 19th century   *Wrest pins:* Original   *Damping:* Mopstick   *Bridge:* Continuous
Action: English single   *Hammer coverings:* Buff leather

There are signs that the instrument was restored in the early part of the present century, at which time the wind pressure was raised. With only a single rise reservoir approximately eighteen inches square and only one feeder operated by a single pedal, it is difficult to keep up a constant supply of air. This situation is further complicated by the additional strain put on the case by the increased pressure needed to fill the reservoir with only the one pedal.

The tone of the organ, however, is very sweet. The lowest forty pipes are mounted transversely and the wind is taken up in channels, grooved on two sides of an oak board covered in leather which runs from the pallet box just below the keyboard. As the channelling has to turn through 90° at the bass end of the instrument there is a weak and vulnerable part of the piano at this point. The treble pipes are planted in the first groove board on the opposite side of the pallet box in the same plane as the keyboard.

The organ is not suitable for the performance of large-scale organ works, but is an interesting small instrument with a pleasing gentle sound designed more for intimate gatherings or, perhaps, continuo work in opera and oratorio. It would have been ideal for the 'Concerts of Ancient Music' in London, whose diet was principally Handel oratorios.

SCHIEDMAYER (STEIN) GRAND

Length: 71″   *Width:* 36¾″
Depth of case: 9⅞″
Height: 28″ (floor to keyboard)
Pedals: Divided *genouillére*
Case: Cherry dyed to simulate mahogany
Legs: Square tapered
Keyboard: Ebony naturals/bone-capped stained beech accidentals
Compass: Five octaves   *Octave size:* 6⅛″
Strings: Replaced   *Wrest pins:* Replaced
Damping: Leather-covered wedges/buff leather
Bridge: Continuous   *Action:* Viennese
Hammer coverings: Buff leather on hollow hammers
Recorded: BBC Archives and Decca, Oryx

not have this refinement. Perhaps because of this adjustment, a check was not thought to be necessary. One of the nightmares of piano restorers is the bother of removing the action again and again for adjustments, with its attendant danger of breaking hammers. This is no problem with the Viennese action, which is much slimmer than its English counterpart. It is also supported on a sledge ('*Schlitten*') which is inserted under the action to raise it to the correct height for playing. To withdraw the action, the lower front board is pulled out, keeping pressure on the action, which drops down to the baseboard when the '*Schlitten*' is removed. In this way there is no danger of hammers being broken or damaged.

The hammers on this piano are all original, and particularly interesting in that they are hollow. In making the hammers hollow, Schiedmayer returned to the method of Cristofori (who made them of rolled parchment covered with leather), but his are leather-covered bamboo. This is one of the few differences between Schiedmayer's pianos and those of his master Stein.

Broadwood square of 1787 with 'elegant' trimmings typical of the period.

8. BROADWOOD GRAND (1787)

Whilst Heilman was writing about Stein from Mainz (see p. 16), John Broadwood was about to make this piano. A superb early Broadwood, it changed hands in about 1920 for the princely sum of twelve shillings, along with other pieces of furniture. After careful restoration it has been recorded by the BBC.

The case is of simple Spanish mahogany (really Cuban, but called Spanish as Cuba was a Spanish colony in the 1780s). It is veneered on oak with boxwood inlay and crossbanded. The lid is solid mahogany with a line of inlay, again in boxwood. As in a harpsichord, the long side of the instrument is unveneered, since the fashion for bringing a piano away from the wall came later, and this side would not have been seen. The stand is a simple mahogany trestle with four plain 'Chippendale' legs which conceal the rods that work the pedal mechanism. The left-side pedal is the '*una corda*' or 'soft' pedal and the right-side one raises the dampers. The ordinary pedal-lyre more readily associated with grand pianos was not adopted by Broadwood until considerably later. The keyboard is made of ivory and ebony and the fronts of the white keys are moulded like cornices – a typical feature of English pianos of the period. Figured maple has been used for the keyboard surround where the maker's name appears:

Johannes Broadwood Londini Fecit 1787

As with harpsichords and early Viennese pianos there is one continuous bridge (see p. 43). Broadwood was concerned about various technical aspects of strings and bridges, and in 1788 patented a double or divided bridge whereby he could bring the bass strings to a better position on the soundboard (see p. 83).

The grain of the soundboard runs parallel with the strings and the wrest pins are unpierced; the majority are original. The instrument is damped throughout and there are fifty-five of the old dampers with their original flannel damping material. Necessary replacements have been made absolutely to the original pattern. The dampers are really only simplified harpsichord jacks, without the tongues and plectra but sliding up and down in grooves exactly as in a harpsichord.

The typical English action numbered 203 appears to have been one of the first 'improved' actions patented in 1783. There are signs of modification – early, not modern – to the action, and there is an ingenious device that allows the distance of the hammers from the strings to be altered merely by adjusting two screws. This is, of course, in addition to the usual refinement of individual adjustment of the set-off from the strings.

BROADWOOD GRAND

Length: 88½″   *Width:* 37¼″   *Depth of case:* 11⅞″   *Height:* 27″ (floor to keyboard)
Pedals: Two wooden – usual functions   *Case:* Spanish mahogany   *Legs:* Square Chippendale type
Keyboard: Ivory naturals/ebony accidentals   *Compass:* Five octaves   *Octave size:* 6⁷⁄₁₆″
Iron hoops: Three (wooden hitchpin plate)   *Strings:* Replaced   *Wrest pins:* Original, unbored   *Damping:* Cloth, original
Bridge: Single continuous   *Action:* English   *Hammer coverings:* Buff leather   *Recorded:* BBC Archives

All the hammers are original, and although fifty-five have been re-leathered the remaining six retain their first leather covering. There is no difference in tone quality between the old and new leather. Piano hammers were re-leathered frequently up till 1840.

One of the most fascinating things about this instrument is the piece of paper that was found behind the nameboard giving full instructions on tuning and regulating (see p. 73).

John Broadwood, born in October 1732 in Cockburnspath in Scotland, was, like Shudi, a carpenter or cabinet maker. He came to London about 1755 and in 1761 found employment in the workshop of Burkat Shudi, who himself had started as a cabinet maker. Thanks to Broadwood's talent and proficiency, he soon became Shudi's best and indispensable assistant. In 1769 he married Shudi's daughter, Barbara, and in the following year became a partner in the business. After his wife's death in 1773, Broadwood was joined by his brother-in-law, Burkat Shudi junior, who withdrew from the business nine years later.

The firm began to think of making pianos in 1773. One of the earliest Broadwood pianos – a square – is dated 1774. A typical early Broadwood square is shown on page 39.

The same Broadwood grand as illustrated on page 41. Note the single continuous bridge reminiscent of a harpsichord of the period.

9. SHUDI-BROADWOOD HARPSICHORD (1790)

This second harpsichord is the last two-manual made by Shudi, who was Kirckman's rival and Broadwood's father-in-law. The last single-manual harpsichord was sent out in 1793, and this instrument pre-dates it by three years.

Burkat Shudi was born on 17 March 1702 in the Canton Glarus in Switzerland. As a sixteen-year-old he came to London and like Kirckman was apprenticed to the Flemish maker Tabel. After about ten years he started his own business, eventually settling in Great Pulteney Street, St James's.

The beautiful casework of this harpsichord is of Spanish mahogany with darker mahogany crossbanding, and the keyboard surround is of satinwood. The registration is basically the same as that of the Kirckman (p. 26), but the instrument is much more sophisticated. On the upper manual the eight-foot strings are quill-plucked, while on the lower a further set of eight-foot strings is leather-plucked. There are four-foot strings and a buff stop. In addition, there is a lute stop on the upper manual. This extra row of jacks plucks the strings nearer the node, giving a nasal sound. But perhaps the most striking feature of Shudi's harpsichord is the 'Venetian Swell' stop. The pianoforte was becoming more and more fashionable by 1780, and harpsichord makers tended to try to imitate its special features. Basically this was impossible, but Shudi's swell, patented in 1769, was a brave effort. Louvres above the string could be gradually opened or closed to let out more or less sound, and without any difference in touch a crescendo or diminuendo could be achieved. Thus a harpsichord fitted with the 'Venetian Swell' could give a sense of expression when required, and this was much appreciated at a time when the subtleties of the piano were not all fully understood.

It has generally been assumed that Kirckman made better-sounding harpsichords than Shudi: more extrovert in tone. But perhaps modern writers have tended to accept Fanny Burney's judgement too readily. An almost exactly similar instrument made by Kirckman, and dating from 1800, is so like the Shudi in touch and tone that either maker could have made either harpsichord. Both Shudi and Kirckman were adhering to the same precepts, and at least to us today there is little appreciable difference between the products of their two workshops.

SHUDI-BROADWOOD HARPSICHORD

Length: 96½″   *Width:* 37½″   *Depth of case:* 12¾″   *Height:* 27½″ (floor to lower keyboard)
Pedals: Two – left machine/right Venetian swell   *Case:* Spanish mahogany crossbanded in mahogany
Legs: Trestle stand – square tapered   *Keyboard:* Ivory naturals/ebony accidentals   *Compass:* Five octaves   *Octave size:* 6⅜″
Strings: Replaced   *Wrest pins:* Original   *Bridge:* Continuous   *Recorded:* Decca

Kirckman two-manual harpsichord of 1800, showing 'Venetian Swell' open. This instrument is very similar to the Shudi-Broadwood of 1790.

The firm of Heilman whose piano began this history were still making beautiful instruments a quarter of a century later – and still with the 'petite' appearance.

10. STEIN GRAND (*c.*1802)

This piano was made by Matthäus Andreas Stein in Vienna. His father, Johann Andreas Georg Stein, who made his reputation in the Fugger town of Augsburg, was a great friend of Leopold Mozart and of his son Wolfgang, both of whom were delighted with his instruments. When the elder Stein died, in 1792, his business was taken over by his son, Matthäus, and his daughter, Nannette. In 1794 these two rather shrewdly moved the firm to Vienna, at that time the Parnassus of music and piano-making. Sadly, their partnership did not last long, and in 1802 they severed business relationships, though they continued manufacturing separately, each under their own name.

This excellent piano was made after the split in the Stein firm. When it first came into the Collection it was in poor condition and needed extensive restoration. The strings had to be replaced and the soundboard had to be removed, repaired and re-installed. The instrument had acquired unauthentic Victorian legs which also needed replacing along with some missing ormolu. The case was otherwise in good condition, charmingly sober with its dark dyed cherrywood.

The compass of the piano is six octaves and the dampers are raised by means of *genouillères* or knee levers. The extensive repairs and restoration have been amply repaid, as this Stein has a clear limpid tone as well as an extremely responsive touch: the success may be heard in a recent recording of Beethoven Songs made by Martin Hill accompanied on this instrument by Christopher Hogwood.

STEIN GRAND

Length: 85½"   *Width:* 45"
Depth of case: 28¾"
Height: 10¼" (floor to keyboard)
Pedals: Genouillére – sustaining
Case: Stained cherry   *Legs:* Square tapered
Keyboard: Bone naturals/ebony-capped stained
  beech accidentals
Compass: 6¼"   *Strings:* Replaced
Wrest pins: Replaced
Damping: Leather wedges to *c'''*, buff leather
  above
Bridge: Continuous   *Action:* Viennese
Hammer coverings: Buff leather
Recorded: Decca

11. ERARD SQUARE (1804)

This charming little piano once belonged to Arnold Dolmetsch. In fact it was the first piano that he ever owned when he was a student in Brussels in about 1880.

In an excellent state, it needed neither repair nor restoration apart from the replacement of half-a-dozen broken strings. The modest, sweet sound makes this instrument ideal for the playing of early music, where its voice blends like that of a powerful clavichord.

The 'dust cover' is in two pieces, unlike the single English one, and the back of the piano is panelled like the front so that it can be positioned in the middle of a room.

The four pedals from left to right activate:

> 1 the bassoon stop
> 2 the damper-raiser
> 3 the moderator
> 4 the pizzicato.

Mario Praz's *Illustrated History of Interior Decoration from Pompeii to Art Nouveau* (Thames and Hudson) has a picture showing Mme Récamier on her famous sofa next to what appears to be a piano exactly like this one.

ERARD SQUARE

Length: 23½″   *Width:* 63″   *Depth of case:* 9½″   *Height:* 27¾″ (floor to keyboard)
Pedals: Four – bassoon/sustain/moderato/buff   *Case:* Mahogany   *Legs:* Turned tapered   *Keyboard:* Ivory naturals/ebony accidentals
Compass: Five-and-a-half octaves *F,–c''''*   *Octave size:* 6¼″   *Strings:* Mainly original   *Wrest pins:* Original
Damping: Mopstick   *Bridge:* Continuous   *Action:* Zumpe's second action   *Hammer coverings:* Buff leather

12. HASCHKA GRAND (*c.*1810)

This elegant Viennese Empire style piano is very similar to one illustrated in Mario Praz' book (see p. 50), which belonged to Napoleon's second wife, Queen Marie Louise (Maria Luiga), and now in the Palazzo Ducale in Parma.

It is not known if Beethoven ever played on a Haschka but he certainly played on a very similar-looking piano in Prague that belonged to Dr Kanka. If this instrument is in any way typical of Haschka's work, his clients certainly did themselves proud. After the battle of the Nile, the most exotic Empire style cases were further garnished with Egyptian motifs. Mechanically this instrument is like so many Viennese pianos of the period that it could have been made by any one of a number of makers. One unusual feature, however, is the veneer on the long side of the instrument, which is extremely simple, suggesting that it was not designed to be shown. In other words, the piano was quite definitely expected to stand against a wall. Otherwise the case is in cherrywood stained to look like mahogany, and the legs were presumably made by Italian craftsmen since the left and right ones are marked in Italian.

Apart from the exotic-looking casework, it is a typical Viennese piano of the period and many hundreds of them were made. The compass of the instrument is six octaves and the stringing is tri-chord throughout. There is a single undivided bridge.

In keeping with the prevailing fashion, the instrument is complete with special effects brought into play by the seven pedals. These, from left to right, bring in:

1 the drum
2 bells and cymbal
3 the moderator
4 the keyboard shift
5 the sustaining pedal
6 the bassoon stop
7 the moderator (as 3, for the other foot).

HASCHKA GRAND

Length: 89"   *Width:* 46½"   *Depth of case:* 10½"   *Height:* 27½" (floor to keyboard)
Pedals: Seven – drum/bells and cymbal/moderato/keyboard shift/sustain/bassoon/alternative moderato   *Case:* Stained cherry
Legs: Four – carved caryatids   *Keyboard:* Bone naturals/stained beech accidentals   *Compass:* Six octaves   *Octave size:* 6¼"
Strings: Replaced   *Wrest pins:* Replaced   *Damping:* Primitive *Kastendämpfung*, plush throughout
Bridge: Continuous   *Action:* Viennese   *Hammer coverings:* Buff leather   *Recorded:* Decca

13. CLEMENTI 'SQUARE' UPRIGHT (1812)

Muzio Clementi was born in Rome in 1752, the son of an embosser of church plate. His first music lessons were from a relation, Signor Buroni, who later became principal composer at St Peter's. At the age of nine the boy was admitted to an organist's post, and by the time he was twelve he was a proficient harpsichordist and composer. Chance, in the shape of the Englishman William Beckford of Fonthill, took over the boy's career at about this time. Beckford had heard of Clementi's genius and managed to prevail upon his parents to allow their son to come to England where he eventually became harpsichordist at the King's Theatre in London.

In 1780 he toured the continent giving recitals on a Shudi harpsichord and on a small square piano, and 1783 found him giving a series of concerts on a pianoforte at the Pantheon in Oxford Street in London.

A change of direction had brought Clementi into the piano manufacturing business when he was induced to take over the bankrupt firm of Longman and Broderip in collaboration with F.W. Collard, the brilliant piano engineer.

In 1802 Clementi visited the Continent for the third time, and stayed abroad for eight years. While in Berlin he married his first wife who died soon afterwards. To get over this shock Clementi visited St Petersburg and then Vienna. In 1807 he agreed, in Vienna, that Beethoven would write three quartets, a symphony, an overture and a violin concerto 'which, at my request, he will adapt for the pianoforte with and without the additional keys', and a piano concerto 'for all of which we are to pay him £200 sterling'. Clementi continued:

> The property, however, is only for the British Dominions . . . I have likewise engaged him to compose two sonatas and a fantasia for the pianoforte which he is to deliver to our house for £60 sterling . . . (mind I have treated for pounds, not guineas).

With such obvious acumen in its founder it is not hard to see why the 'house' of Clementi and Collard flourished!

In 1810 Clementi returned to England, and married again in the following year. At this time he also published his highly successful and practical 'Gradus ad Parnassum' – a series of pianoforte studies.

Muzio Clementi died in Evesham in 1832 after, so it is said, an affaire with a washer-woman – a species he pursued with great devotion! He was buried in the cloisters of Westminster Abbey with all the ceremony due to 'the Father of the Pianoforte'.

CLEMENTI 'SQUARE' UPRIGHT

Length: 19¾″   *Width:* 55½″
Height of case: 59½″
Height: 27½″ (floor to keyboard)
Pedals: Mahogany   *Legs:* Turned reeded
Keyboard: Ivory naturals/ebony accidentals
Compass: Six octaves   *Octave size:* 6½″
Strings: Replaced   *Wrest pins:* Original
Damping: Cloth   *Bridge:* Continuous
Action: Clementi's own upright, not sticker
Hammer coverings: Buff leather

Although Clementi's name appears below the keyboard of this instrument, it is obviously a 'bought in' make.

Opening the front of the instrument reveals a square piano simply turned on its side (Collard patented this in 1811). This represents a somewhat unsuccessful effort to make an upright piano and thus to save floor space – unsuccessful because the space actually saved is minimal.

The casework of the piano is very elegant indeed with its ionic pilasters, ormolu dancing maidens and brass gallery. The six-octave compass is larger than usual for an instrument of this date, but the single sustaining pedal is perfectly in period.

The tuning pins are placed on the right-hand side of the piano, as they were in most 'non-Broadwood' squares of the time, but the stringing is of course diagonal, which baffles the tuner used to early square pianos, since the wrest pins tuning the bass are on the top right and those for the treble are on the bottom right – exactly the reverse of what he is used to.

The action is surprisingly sophisticated, and seems to antedate Wornum's, but the dampers, though very efficient, are activated from the back of the piano, which makes them difficult to adjust.

The instrument has been carefully restored and now sounds exactly like a square piano of the same date. One unusual feature is that the extreme bass notes are monochord, much like those on Pleyel's pianos twenty years later (see p. 110). A very similar instrument is to be found in the Gothenburg Museum.

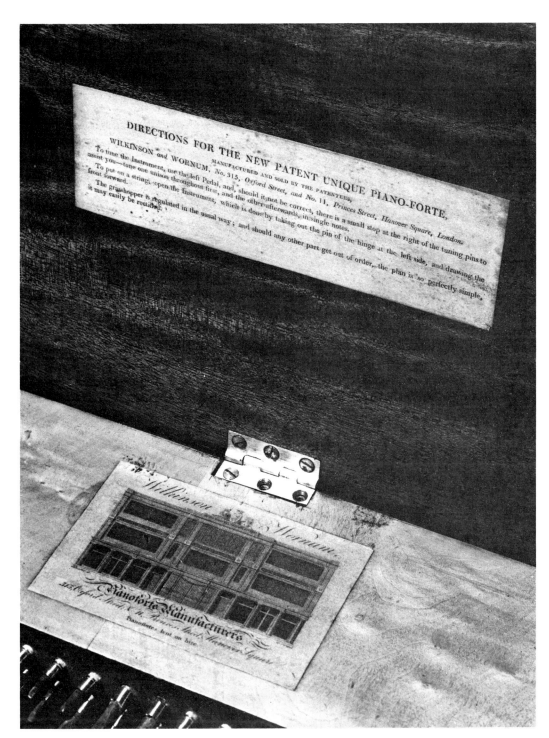

Nameplate and printed instructions for tuning a cottage piano by Wilkinson and Wornum, *c.* 1811.

14. WILKINSON AND WORNUM UPRIGHT (*c.*1812)

This exquisite little upright piano must be one of the earliest English 'pianinos' in existence. It has been suggested that Wilkinson and Wornum joined forces in 1796 after the demise of Longman and Broderip. However, Clementi was able to pick up some of the pieces of that illustrious firm in 1800 (see p. 54), so it may be that Wilkinson and Wornum did not start making pianos until later than has been supposed.

The instrument has a number of unusual features for such an early upright piano. The two pedals are somewhat deceptive since the left-side one acts only as a damper on the left-hand strings (the piano is bi-chord throughout) for the purposes of tuning. It is not a 'buff' or 'moderator' stop. The right-side pedal, on the other hand, is a perfectly straightforward damper-raiser.

The stringing is diagonal to allow greater length in a small space, and the compass is the usual five-and-a-half octaves. Wornum had patented a very similar 'improved' upright in 1811, with the diagonal strings, and a buff stopping one string of each note, worked by a pedal.

The piano was obviously designed to be placed in the middle of a room if desired, and not only against a wall, because great care has been taken with the veneering of the back, even to the extent that rosewood crossbanding in keeping with the rest of the instrument has been applied. The keyboard flap is not hinged, as one would have expected, but quite loose so that it can be removed entirely. Such a piano could have been used at sea without the pianist's hands being broken by a falling keyboard cover in choppy weather. A small strut allows the lid to be propped open to allow more sound out, and inside it there are instructions for tuning and regulating the instrument (p. 57) and a small leather thong to hold the tuning key. Just below the elegant keyboard there is a cunningly concealed drawer for music. The two mirrors appear to be original but the old pleated silk has had to be replaced with moiré taffeta.

WILKINSON & WORNUM UPRIGHT

Length: 47½"   *Width:* 19"
Height of case: 41"
Height: 30" (floor to keyboard)
Pedals: Two – sustaining/buff muting one string
   for tuning
Case: Mahogany crossbanded in rosewood
Legs: Two – turned reeded
Keyboard: Ivory naturals/ebony accidentals
Compass: Five-and-a-half octaves
Octave size: 6⅜"   *Strings:* Replaced
Wrest pins: Original   *Damping:* Cloth
Bridge: Continuous
Action: Wornum's tape check (a later alteration)
Hammer coverings: Buff leather

15.   CLEMENTI UPRIGHT GRAND (1816)

Anyone frustrated in trying to get hold of an eighteenth-century grand piano would be well advised to settle for an instrument like this one. Although it was built in 1816, the tone of this Clementi is exactly that of an eighteenth-century grand – even throughout its whole five-and-a-half octave range, sonorous in the bass and strong and clear in the treble. Since the sound is surely the most important aspect of any musical instrument, music-lovers will be bound to forgive the upright grand's rather freakish appearance.

The Clementi stands some 8′3″ high on its original castors, and even by Victorian standards is a large piece of furniture. It is hardly surprising that many upright grand pianos had to have their legs shortened to be installed. Like a square piano, this one sits on a stand supported by four reeded legs. The two pedals are also fixed to this stand. They function as modern piano pedals – the right-side pedal raising the dampers and the left-side one shifting the keyboard for the *una corda* ('one string' only being hit, therefore making a softer sound).

The keyboard surround is in satinwood, as is the lining of the drop cylinder front. The name 'Clementi & Co., 112, Cheapside, London' is painted in gold and surrounded by an elegant floral arrangement.

This instrument makes an interesting comparison with a later Stodart piano (see p. 63). The Stodart's date is hard to read, but would appear to be 1823. When closed the instrument looks exactly like a bureau bookcase, and the keyboard cover gives the impression of being a pull-out drawer. Anyone not noticing the pedals might be forgiven for expecting to find the usual secretaire furnishings inside it! Stodart had patented a 'bookcase' upright, in which both hammers and dampers returned by weights, as early as 1795, about the time when the first upright grands were made in England.

CLEMENTI UPRIGHT GRAND

Length: 23¼″   *Width:* 42½″
Height of case: 103″
Height: 28¼″ (floor to keyboard)
Pedals: Two – usual functions
Case: Mahogany
Legs: Trestle stand – four turned reeded legs
Keyboard: Ivory naturals/ebony accidentals
Compass: Five-and-a-half octaves
Octave size: 6⅜″   *Iron hoops:* Four
Strings:: Original except brass strings
Wrest pins:: Original   *Damping:* Cloth
Bridge: Divided
Action: English upright grand, no stickers
Hammer coverings: Buff leather replacements
Recorded: BBC Archives

Another Clementi upright grand of 1816. With the doors open one can see the instrument's construction.

Stodart upright grand, *c.* 1820. These
upright grands were very tall, over 100″,
about 8′4″ or more.

63

16. DULCKEN GRAND (1816)

The Flemish had always been great makers of keyboard instruments – especially harpsichords – but were not particularly enamoured of the 'modern' pianos. Born in Amsterdam, Dulcken was a descendant of the better-known harpsichord-maker, Ludwig. Already a celebrated harpsichord maker, he moved south to more congenial 'piano' climes and in 1785 achieved the post of '*Hof Klaviermacher*' to Kurfürst Karl Theodore of Munich. It is interesting that a modern Dutch maker has turned his hand to copying Dulcken instruments.

The unusual feature of this piano is a 'dummy' soundboard, which has been the cause of some controversy: some call it a dust cover. This it is not. It is a simple device to muffle the sound and to kill all traces of action noise. Naturally it helps to produce a sweeter and more lush sound which is dispelled the moment the 'dust cover' is removed. Perhaps Wagner had something of the sort in mind when he put his orchestra at Bayreuth into a covered pit.

This typically German fortepiano has a Viennese action, a walnut-veneered case and fine tapered legs. The compass of the instrument is six octaves and the keys are covered with bone rather than ivory. The accidentals are in stained beech capped with ebony.

The elegant lyre supports four pedals:

     1 a keyboard shift
     2 a bassoon stop which affects only the extreme bass notes
     3 a moderator which inserts a woollen cloth between the strings and the hammers
     4 a damper-raiser.

Most pianos of this period were tri-chord, with perhaps a few bass bi-chords, but Dulcken's instrument is bi-chord almost throughout. This naturally makes tuning a shorter job, and the loss of volume is amply made up for by the use of thicker strings.

The three iron struts in the frame are situated under the soundboard and are hidden by three sets of dummy strings so that the observer can see no break in the symmetry of the layout.

DULCKEN GRAND

Length: 91″   *Width:* 46″   *Depth of case:* 12″   *Height:* 28½″ (floor to keyboard)
Pedals: Four – bassoon/keyboard shift/moderato/sustain   *Case:* Walnut   *Legs:* Square tapered
Keyboard: Bone naturals/stained beech accidentals   *Compass:* Six octaves   *Octave size:* 6¼″   *Strings:* Replaced
Wrest pins: Original   *Damping:* Leather-covered to c''', buff (*Kastendämpfung*) above
Bridge: Single continuous   *Action:* Viennese   *Hammer coverings:* Buff leather   *Recorded:* Decca

17. ERARD GRAND (1818)

Sebastien Erard was descended from a German family, Erhardt, and was born on 5 April 1752 in Strasbourg, Alsace, the son of a carpenter. At the age of sixteen he came to Paris as an apprentice to a *clavecin* maker, but soon surpassed his master and was, therefore, dismissed. The reputation of his outstanding skill spread so quickly that after a very short time he attracted the attention of the aristocracy, and in 1776 he found a patroness in the Duchesse de Villeroi who appreciated his art and gave him suitable rooms for setting up a workshop in her castle. Here, in 1777, he finished the first pianoforte ever made in France. Together with his brother Jean Baptiste Erard he founded his own establishment in the rue de Bourbon in Paris. The rapidly growing reputation of the firm made it possible for the brothers to found a branch in London in 1786 and they stayed here during the French Revolution.

Numerous innovations and inventions in the construction of the instruments are inseparably connected with the name of Erard. Especially worth mentioning is his '*piano organisé*', the '*harpe à fourchette*', the '*orgue expressif*' and particularly the double pedal harp ('*à double mouvement*') of 1811.

This Erard Grand, from the Paris factory, has a very beautiful lyre with ormolu mounts and five pedals as well as a sideways-moving *genouillère* which works a drum built into the bottom of the bass of the instrument. Taken from left to right the pedals produce the same 'effects' as Erard's square of 1804 (p. 50):

1 pizzicato, as if the string is plucked as in a harpsichord (buff leather pressed against the strings)

2 bassoon – a 'reedy' sound (parchment pressed against the strings)

3 moderator – a mellow sound (cloth placed between the strings and the hammers)

4 sustained sound (the dampers raised) and one extra facility as on the Dulcken of 1816 (p. 64)

5 *una corda* (the keyboard shifted to the left so that the hammers strike one string only – a quieter sound).

The very plain mahogany casework has been so carefully chosen that no other decoration is necessary except for six very beautiful and well-worked pieces of ormolu. The turned mahogany tapered legs with ormolu caps and feet are typically French. The keyboard has ivory naturals and ebony accidentals, the former supported on a boxwood cornice, very similar to the English ones. The keyboard flap, when lifted, reveals a beautifully written name-*etiquette* and folds back flush so that one is unaware of any keyboard covering. Although it has been re-strung, the piano still retains most of the original dampers and all the original hammer facings. The hammers themselves are very flat –

ERARD GRAND

Length: 80″   *Width:* 43″   *Depth of case:* 10¾″   *Height:* 28″ (floor to keyboard)
Pedals: Five – buff/bassoon/moderato/sustain/*una corda*, also *genouillère* (drum)   *Case:* Mahogany
Legs: Three – turned tapered   *Keyboard:* Ivory naturals/ebony accidentals   *Compass:* Six octaves   *Octave size:* 6⅜″
Iron hoops: Five   *Strings:* Replaced   *Wrest pins:* Original   *Damping:* Cloth   *Bridge:* Divided
Action: Erard's first repetition (see Harding)   *Hammer coverings:* Buff leather   *Recorded:* Decca

not through wear, but because they were so designed. Many people imagine that a hammer must be pointed, but in fact many early makers preferred a flat surface to hit the strings.

Technically the Erard Grand is one of the most exciting instruments in the Collection. Although its compass is small – only six octaves – the action is most sophisticated, antedating most others of the type by about fifty years. The instrument is dated 1818, but it is known that Erard patented a repetition action as early as 1808. It is sad that Beethoven's Erard which he found so unsatisfactory was presented to him in 1804. If only he had waited another four years he would certainly have owned a piano that would have satisfied and impressed him.

The touch of this piano is surprisingly light and the repetition is extremely rapid. This is also a feature of Viennese pianos of the period, but in their case a key could not be used to repeat a note without first fully returning to the attack position. With the Erard it is possible to repeat a note rapidly even if it is half-way depressed, which is, of course one of the foremost prerequisites of a good piano action. This certainly was a good action, if a bit cumbersome, and Erard later simplified it and in about 1820 produced an action (patented by Pierre Erard in 1921) that formed the basis of modern piano actions some fifty years in advance of all other makers.

This particular Erard came into the Collection under a cloak of secrecy since its original owner did not wish her relatives to know that the instrument had been sold. There can be no doubt, however, that it is more likely to survive in its present situation than it was in the remote Hebridean castle whence it came and where it was never played.

By 1812 the elegance of Broadwood squares had taken in the new decorative fashion. The reader may care to compare this with the square illustrated on page 39.

18. BROADWOOD GRAND (1819)

This instrument, no. 8074, was made in 1819 by John Broadwood, the great English piano manufacturer. Broadwood made about 4,000 similar pianofortes between 1808 and 1820, and it was just such a model that he sent to Beethoven in 1816.

The Beethoven piano, which is now in Budapest, had to make a much longer journey than the one illustrated. It was sent by ship to Trieste and then overland to Vienna – a distance of almost 1,000 miles. The fact that it arrived safely bears witness to the extraordinary care with which the instruments were packed. They were first wrapped in soft leather covers and then put into secondary cases made of deal and lined with zinc. To protect the moulding on the legs, these were covered with specially knitted socks! Such niceties must have come as second nature to Broadwood, who exported his pianos as far afield as Russia, Calcutta and even the West Indies.

The casework of this instrument is somewhat more elegant than that of Beethoven's, the 'plum-pudding' mahogany veneer being set off by fine rosewood crossbanding. The lid is secured by three gilt cast-brass drop-handles and the legs are made of carefully-chosen mahogany with some ebonised mouldings. The whole is easily moved on its original castors.

The ivory and ebony keyboard is surrounded by rosewood richly inlaid with brass, and the boxwood nameboard reads:

John Broadwood & Sons Maker to His Majesty and the Princesses,
Gt Pulteney Street, Golden Square, London.

An original lyre of the period was the model for this very carefully copied one. The right-side sustaining pedal is split into two, one half acting on the lower (bass) half of the keyboard and the other on the treble. This refinement, typical of the instruments of the period, is a precursor of the 'third' pedal on modern concert grand pianos. Needless to say, both halves of the pedal can be depressed at once by a carefully positioned foot. In addition to the 'soft' pedal, there is a handstop at the right of the keyboard which shifts it to the right so that only one of the three strings is hit – for true *una corda* playing.

With the exception of the top eighteen notes of the piano, the original strings – some one hundred and sixty years old – have been retained, though the pitch of the instrument is consequently one semitone lower than that of modern pianos.

In comparison with others of the period the Broadwood pianoforte boasts an immense sonority in

BROADWOOD GRAND

Length: 97″ *Width:* 44″ *Depth of case:* 11½″ *Height:* 28″ (floor to keyboard)
Pedals: Two – one split (usual functions) *Case:* Mahogany veneer/rosewood crossbanding/gilt brass handles
Legs: Four – turned mahogany with ebonised moulding – brass castors *Keyboard:* Ivory naturals/ebony accidentals
Compass: Six octaves *Octave size:* 6⅜″ *Iron hoops:* Five *Strings:* Original *Wrest pins:* Original *Damping:* White flannel
Bridge: Divided *Action:* Broadwood English *Hammer coverings:* Leather/doeskin, soft *Recorded:* BBC Archives

the bass, which, with the greater than normal touch depth, undoubtedly appealed enormously to Beethoven who by 1816 was so deaf as to *feel* tone rather than hear it. Contemporary reports avow that he was delighted with the 'rough-toned' instrument, although most continental musicians vastly preferred the Viennese pianos with their brighter treble, better damping, more even tone and lightness of touch.

An interesting note in the Porters' Book for Broadwood sheds more light on this particular instrument:

Friday June 11th 1819 – no. 8074 –
Stukey – a six octave Grand Piano, Broadwood no. 8074 for Mr Calmisac, delivered at:
Mr Stukey, 126 Sloane Street – bringing a Broadwood Square Piano no. 23781 from ditto.

This seems to show that Broadwood clients enjoyed the facility of 'part-exchange'.

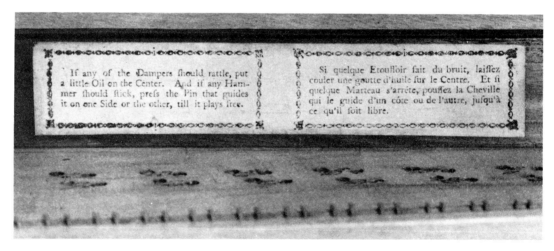

Broadwoods exported many early pianos to France. Hence the bi-lingual instructions provided on one of 1787.

DIRECTIONS for TUNING, and KEEPING the GRAND PIANO FORTE in ORDER.

FIRST, turn up the small Piece of Wood which is fixed upon the Block, on the treble Side of the Keys, and putting down the left Pedal, the Hammers will strike on one Unison, which tune as you do the Harpsichord; then turn down the said Piece of Wood, and putting down again the left Pedal, the Hammers will strike on two Unisons, which tune; and lastly, by letting the Pedal go, you may tune the third Unison to the other two.

As for the Hammers, they ought to have just Freedom enough to fall easy; for if they have too much Freedom, they will rattle; if too little, they will stick. These may be regulated by gently turning with a Pair of Pliers, or a Tool made for the Purpose, the little Screw with a square Head, which goes into the Head of each Hammer; or, by drawing out the Keys, which is done by unscrewing the two Screws that pass through the Bottom of the Piano Forte into the Blocks on each Side of the Keys, and then turning with a Screw-driver the said little Screws. But great Care must be taken, that the Hammers do not suffer in taking the Keys out, or in putting them in again.

As the Hammers ought to rise within half a quarter of an Inch of the String before they fall down, to regulate them in this Respect, there is a long Pin to every Key, like those that the Strings are tuned by, which by screwing in, with a Tuning-hammer, makes the Hammer fall sooner; and, by unscrewing, makes the Hammer rise nearer the String.

But if it should be required to raise or lower all the Hammers, it may be done at once by the smallest Turn of the two Pins of the same length, fixed in Plates on each Side of the Keys.

N.B. If the Hammers rise too near the String, they knock; and if they fall too soon, they speak too soft.

In most early Broadwood 'large' pianos there were printed instructions on how to adjust the action. Those above appear in an instrument of 1787.

19. KIRKMAN GRAND (1820)

The same Kirchmann, an Alsatian, who changed his name to Kirckman when he came to England (see p. 26), changed it once again to Kirkman when he started to make grand pianos. An inventory of the furniture in the Brighton Pavilion made in 1833 mentions a patent grand piano by Kirkman. Unfortunately the illustrations in the archives are not as clear as that of the Tomkison grand piano in the Entrance Hall (see p. 78). It is therefore impossible to be absolutely certain that this instrument is in fact a royal one. However, the beauty of the workmanship and the unusually elegant casework would certainly have fitted it for such an exalted residence. The King was not shy about his love of music and of furniture, and the Kirkman piano would have appealed to him both as an instrument and as a decorative feature. The exquisite rosewood case, although much simpler than that of the Tomkison is nevertheless extremely elegant and the instrument has some unusual mechanical features.

Seeking to emulate the octave stop of the harpsichord, Kirkman gave his piano an extra bridge. The layout of this bridge is complicated. When the keyboard shift pedal is depressed, the hammers move to the right and only play on the eight-foot strings. When the pedal is released, however, the hammers strike both the eight-foot strings and another set of four-foot strings, which sound an octave higher. This gives a sound totally different from that of any contemporary piano – plummy, full and very brilliant; an extraordinary combination. Kirkman had patented this 'octave stop' in 1816.

The instrument is difficult to keep in tune and inclined to be unstable. George IV, however, undoubtedly had a full-time piano tuner at the Pavilion and such considerations would not have worried him.

KIRKMAN GRAND

Length: 92½″   *Width:* 44½″   *Depth of case:* 12¼″   *Height:* 27½″ (floor to keyboard)
Pedals: Two – usual functions   *Case:* Figured rosewood   *Legs:* Trestle stand – four turned reeded legs
Keyboard: Ivory naturals/ebony accidentals   *Compass:* Six octaves   *Octave size:* 6⅜″   *Iron hoops:* Six   *Strings:* Replaced
Wrest pins: Replaced   *Damping:* Cloth   *Bridge:* Divided, with octave undivided bridge in addition
Action: English grand: *Hammer coverings:* Buff leather

20. TOMKISON GRAND (1821)

This opulent and lavishly decorated piano definitely had a royal owner. When it came into the Collection it badly needed cleaning, and when the action was removed, there in Indian ink was a simple note:

For the King, December 21st 1821.

Further research led to the Brighton Pavilion and eventually to a Nash illustration of the entrance hall to that extravagant pile. There, looking perfectly at home, was the Tomkison Grand which now rubs cases with pianos of all ages and classes (p. 78).

However, the Tomkison is not quite alone. In 1949 a rather dirty-looking Broadwood grand came into the Collection. Over the last thirty years it has been carefully restored. Its serial number is identifiable: no. 8948. A recent search in the porter's books at the firm of Broadwood uncovered the truth:

His Majesty – an elegant six octave grand piano in rio (Rio Rosewood)
185 guineas – no. 8948 – delivered at His Majesty George IV's Pavilion, Brighton

If, as I believe, the Kirkman shown on page 75 is indeed the one referred to in the 1833 inventory, all three Brighton Pavilion pianos have at last come to rest in the same music room after some one hundred and fifty years.

Of the three 'Pavilion' pianos, the Tomkison is, perhaps, the strangest in design. While the other two are fairly straightforward, this one has legs reminiscent of an earlier era. They are carved out of solid rosewood and reflect Renaissance taste rather than the oriental splendour of the Brighton Pavilion interior. The rest of the casework, on the other hand, is perfectly in keeping with the marine residence.

Thomas Tomkison was a very distinguished piano builder who only started in business between 1798 and 1800. His workshop was at 55 Dean Street, Soho, and there he was one of the first to produce an 'overstrung' instrument. The substantial fortune that he made allowed him to retire in about 1840 and to enjoy his considerable fine art collection. Tomkison pianos are characterised by their unusually fine casework, and it would appear that he made very few uprights. Two only survive and were probably bought in and sold under his name. One of them has been in the Brussels Conservatoire Collection since before 1910.

TOMKISON GRAND

Length: 96½″   *Width:* 46½″   *Depth of case:* 11½″   *Height:* 27″ (floor to keyboard)
Pedals: Two – usual functions   *Case:* Rosewood with elaborate brass inlay   *Legs:* Three – decorated inverted lyres
Keyboard: Ivory naturals/ebony accidentals   *Compass:* Six octaves   *Octave size:* 6⅜″   *Iron hoops:* Five
Strings: Replaced   *Wrest pins:* Replaced   *Damping:* Cloth dampers to *b′* flat only   *Bridge:* Divided
Action: Broadwood-type English   *Hammer coverings:* Buff leather

Interior view of the Entrance Hall in the Brighton Pavilion by Nash, showing the second 'Pavilion' piano, described on page 76.

The third 'Pavilion' piano, described in the Broadwood porters' books.

21. BROADWOOD COTTAGE (*c.* 1825)

This piano with its magnificent rosewood case lavishly inlaid with brass would surely have been more likely to grace a lady's boudoir than an artisan's cottage!

There are the usual two pedals, keyboard shift on the left, and the sustaining pedal on the right. Pianos of this period, on the Continent especially, could have their pedals either way around, but in England, where a multiplicity of pedals never became popular, grand pianos always had the *una corda* pedal on the left and the sustaining pedal on the right. English pianos, with the exception of those of the maker Wornum, were also consistent in that the keyboard always shifted to the right.

The legs of this impressive upright piano are exquisitely turned and are capped with gilt brass ferrules. The moiré silk front is new. When it first came into the Collection in 1962 it had a rather beautiful faded silk of an inexpressibly lovely lavender colour, which, sadly, was too worn to be retained and also, apparently, impossible to duplicate.

Mechanically, the piano is in its original condition. The hammers and dampers still retain their original coverings and the wrest pins have not been rebored. Because this piano has no ironwork in its frame, and because practically all the strings are original, the instrument has been kept a semitone below modern pitch. It is interesting to note, too, that all the stringing is bi-chord – two strings and not three to every note – such as Broadwood had begun to introduce into grands as well as uprights about this time (see p. 149), besides improvements like the check action for squares and metal string plate for grands patented in 1825 and 1827 respectively.

John Broadwood remained the sole owner of the firm 'Shudi and Broadwood' until 1795, when he took his son James Shudi Broadwood as a partner. The name of the firm was then changed to 'John Broadwood and Son'. The plural name 'John Broadwood and Sons' dates from 1807 when a son from a later marriage, Thomas Broadwood, entered as the third partner. John Broadwood, whose eponymous products acquired a world-wide reputation, died in 1812. His son James (1772-1851) outlived him by nearly forty years. After James's death the business passed on to his son, Henry Fowler Broadwood (1811-1893).

In 1788 the firm had succeeded in bringing onto the market improved grand pianos with 'balanced scaling'. This was a method of giving a more sonorous bass to the instrument and also, incidentally, a shorter case. It was achieved by splitting the bridge into two and putting the bass strings higher up on the soundboard. This system was soon copied by other makers (and in 1821 Collard even patented a third bridge, to allow the part of the strings generally damped to vibrate in unison with the lengths

BROADWOOD COTTAGE

Length: 22¼″   *Width:* 42½″
Height of case: 47½″
Height: 27½″ (floor to keyboard)
Pedals: Two – usual functions
Case: Rosewood with brass inlay
Legs: Two – turned tapered
Keyboard: Ivory naturals/ebony accidentals
Compass: Five-and-a-half octaves
Octave size: 6⅜″   *Strings:* Original
Damping: Cloth   *Bridge:* Continuous
Action: Sticker   *Hammer coverings:* Buff leather

between the ordinary bridges – like the Bluthner Aliquot scale). But there were still many Continental pianos which stuck to the 'Viennese' model of an undivided bridge and, consequently, a longer case. One such Continental piano was made in Vienna by Haschka in 1825.

Water-colour sketch of Thomas Broadwood, _c._ 1820, by an unknown artist, kindly presented to the author by Miss C.Broadwood.

The divided bridge seen on an earlier Broadwood grand.

22. HASCHKA GRAND (*c.* 1825)

The early nineteenth century craze for special effects and, particularly, for percussion imitating the 'Turkish' music of the military bands was unabated in 1825, the year before the 'Janissaries' (the Sultan's bodyguard) finally revolted against their master. Janissary bands depended on drums, bells and cymbals. Erard had built in a drum in his 1818 grand: Haschka went one better, with one pedal working a drum under the soundboard, three bells *and* a cymbal clash on the bottom octave of the strings. The four remaining pedals worked in the same way as Erard's, producing *una corda*, bassoon, sustainment and moderator.

The shape of the case too is unusual in this instrument: the long side is triple bent, a feature of design that found a certain favour between 1810 and 1825. The wood used is a highly decorative walnut whose pattern has been chosen to give the appearance of moths' wings. The three sturdy legs are in the shape of doric columns and are decorated with gesso (a kind of Plaster of Paris) and gilt. The leg at the tail of the instrument has been disconcertingly placed just off centre, so that it looks unsteady unless the piano is placed against a wall.

The action is typically Viennese with no adjustment screws, and all the hammers retain their original leather coverings which gives the piano a splendid authentic tone – the perfect foil for the human voice. When this magnificent instrument came into the Collection, there was no maker's name apparent on it. Assiduous searching, however, revealed a scribble under the wrest plank: Georg Haschka.

Almost nothing is known of Haschka. He was born in about 1772 in the then Austrian province of Moravia in Czechoslovakia and died in Vienna early in 1828. In 1818 he was working '*Am Neubau 232*' and in 1820 '*Am Neubau Holzplatzl. 140*'. It is uncertain whether his business was closed on his death or whether it was taken on by one of his five children.

The illustration on p. 86 shows Rossini's first wife, the singer Isabella Colbran, seated at an uncannily similar instrument made by Franz Wehrle, the Viennese maker. Wehrle sought permission to set up a business in Vienna in 1815, and there are records of his living near Graf's workshop in 1817. Apart from that, and the fact that one of his pianos has been immortalised in this painting by Waldmüller, Wehrle is as shadowy a figure as Haschka.

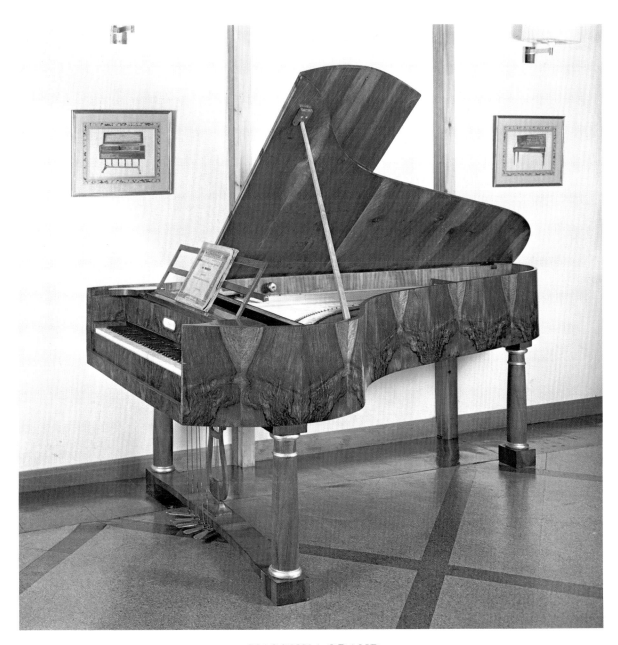

HASCHKA GRAND

Length: 94½″   *Width:* 51½″   *Depth of case:* 12¾″   *Height:* 29″ (floor to keyboard)
Pedals: Five – keyboard shift/bassoon/sustaining/moderato/Turkish music   *Case:* Walnut   *Legs:* Three – turned columns
Keyboard: Bone naturals/stained beech accidentals   *Compass:* Six-and-a-half octaves C_1–g'''' *Octave size:* 6¼″
Strings: Replaced   *Wrest pins:* Original   *Damping:* Leather-covered wedges, buff leather pads above (*Kastendämpfung*)
Bridge: Continuous   *Action:* Viennese   *Hammer coverings:* Buff leather   *Recorded:* Decca and BBC Archives

Rossini's first wife seated at an
instrument by Wehrle very similar to
the 1825 Haschka. By courtesy of the
Haus der Kunst, Munich.

Broadwood grand of 1824 showing iron tension bars as described on page 148.

23.   TWO CLEMENTI SQUARES (*c.* 1825)

Both these charming Clementis came into the Collection in about 1960.

To start with the more eye-catching of the two, the brass inlay is so grand and costly that one cannot help wondering whether it was made for somebody very important indeed. It must be one of the most elaborate square pianos ever made. The rosewood case is covered with inlaid figures of dancing maidens and 'Pan' characters at the rounded corners. It is interesting that the compass of the instrument is larger than usual for the period – six-and-a-half octaves. There can be no doubt that this was an especially commissioned piano. The 'additional notes' had been considered by Clementi for some years, as his commission to Beethoven in 1807 indicates, and as several composers wrote on their title pages:

Both pianos have two pedals. In each case the left-side one raises the dampers and the right-side one raises a second damper which rests on the unused length of the strings to the right of the bridge. This device, patented by Stewart in 1821, antedated Bluthner's 'Aliquot' scale by something like a

CLEMENTI SQUARE

Length: 26¼″   *Width:* 72″   *Depth of case:* 13″   *Height:* 29½″ (floor to keyboard)
Pedals: Two – sustaining/harmonic swell   *Case:* Rosewood, brass inlay   *Legs:* Six – turned reeded
Keyboard: Ivory naturals/ebony accidentals   *Compass:* Six-and-a-half octaves   *Octave size:* 6⅜″   *Strings:* Original
Wrest pins: Original   *Damping:* Dolly dampers   *Bridge:* Continuous   *Action:* English double
Hammer coverings: Buff leather   *Recorded:* BBC Archives

hundred years. The effect of raising this second damper was to produce sympathetic vibration – and the stop was known as a 'harmonic' swell (see p. 91). The pleasant echo effect achieved was much appreciated by Clementi, who used the device in some of his grand pianos as well.

The less ornate of the two pianos (p. 91) is housed in a case of Cuban mahogany crossbanded with rosewood. The six legs are of mahogany, reeded and with gilt brass ferrules on the top and finely-made castors at the bottom. This piano also boasts three drawers for music – an echo of the design of the Kirckman harpsichord (p. 27). The brass handles to these drawers are of top quality and the dust cover inside the lid is highly decorated with silver flowers on a green background.

Unlike its grander sister, this square boasts only the more usual six-octave compass. The natural keys are of ivory on boxwood and the accidentals are of ebony. The nameboard is pierced to the right and left with decorative fretwork, and the name itself is painted in gold and other colours with sprigs of flowers and a crown. There is also a modest amount of brass inlay.

When this piano was bought it seemed desperately low in pitch, and on further examination it was found to be suffering from a severe defect: the main part of the instrument was parting company with the bottom! As the piano had all its original strings, dampers, hammers and hammer coverings quite untouched, it was a problem to know just what ought to be done. Finally, after careful planning, the strings were let down and the case was gently clamped up for one week. Since no further damage was apparent, the clamps were released and more than usual liquid fish glue was squirted into the gap which was then quickly re-clamped. With the addition of a few long screws, the repair was effected and the piano still keeps in very good tune with its base-board now firmly in place. It was recorded for BBC Archives by Ruth Dyson.

The Metropolitan Museum contains an instrument almost exactly like this one – even down to the brass handles – under the name of Alpheus Babcock, which suggests that this, too, was in fact manufactured by Clementi and sold with Babcock's name on it. This was common practice at the time. Indeed, Clementi also 'bought in' other makes and sold them under his own name. One can never be quite sure 'what's in a name?' On page 92 is a good example. This beautifully painted nameboard appears on a square piano by William Rolfe. The firm of Rolfe made pianos from 1785 until 1888 and had a reputation for good instruments. The fascinating thing about this nameboard, however, is that the identical design of flowers appears on another instrument by a different maker – the 1816 Clementi upright grand shown on page 61, complete with the highly ornate nameboard. On

Clementi square, *c*. 1822, showing 'Harmonic Swell'.

the upright piano, the design is slightly larger, but otherwise it is exactly the same. This is a perfect example of the eighteenth and nineteenth century pattern book 'choice' that was available to purchasers, who could add their own name if they so wished – maker, dealer, or even owner. Decorative surrounds such as this were quite common on square pianos, but by no means so on grands, which makes the Clementi upright the more unusual. As one would expect, the design has been hand-painted in oils, and the music-loving botanist will quickly spot everlasting sweet peas, *rosa centifolia*, convolvulus, Turk's cap lilies and blue auriculas in this charming garland.

William Rolfe and Sons claim they are 'real manufacturers' in their 'Directions for Regulating the Patent Double Action Pianoforte' – a forerunner of the advertisements 'Beware of Imitations'.

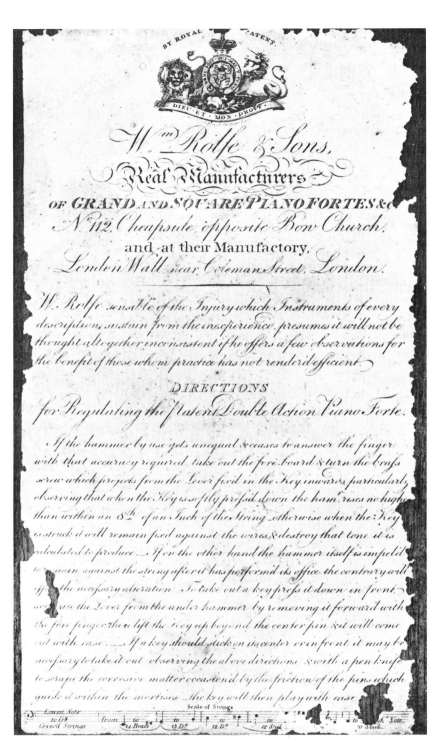

Instructions regarding the adjustment of a Rolfe square, *c.* 1820.

24. SCHLEIP LYRAFLÜGEL (1825)

'Buying-in' actions and putting them – or indeed putting makers' own actions – into different shapes and designs of frame produced some lovely and some unlovely furniture. Schleip's design for a superb upright piano incorporated a Wornum-type action and an Empire style case. It found many imitators, and became *démodé* only in the 1850s. Makers by then could bring the strings down to the floor which enabled them to produce an upright instrument less than five feet in height.

This splendid instrument (which also appears on the jacket) has 'the additional keys' making the extraordinary compass *D,* to *g''''*. The hammers are leather-covered and very flat where they strike the strings. Most curious of all, the soundboard is free-standing – not fixed to the framework at all, but free to vibrate with the obliquely laid strings.

There are three *genouillères* or knee-levers instead of pedals, giving, from left to right:

       1 a bassoon stop (still by applying a sheet of parchment to the strings)

       2 the keyboard shift

       3 the usual damper-raiser.

All the original strings exist and the keyboard is beautifully worked in thick ivory with chamfered edges and very long ebony accidentals.

A similar Austrian piano has quite a different layout. Although it looks superficially the same, the beautifully grained rosewood front is, in fact, the soundboard, and the hammers hit the strings from the back of the case. Whereas the wrest pins in the Schleip instrument are on the right-hand side following the curve of the lyre, in this one they are in front of the player, just behind the keyboard. As we can see, there was still a fondness for decorative uprights in the 1840s.

This 'Giraffenflügel', *c.* 1840, has the unusually large compass of seven octaves $C_{,,}-c''''$. Probably made by Ehrlich of Bamberg, it once belonged to Dr Helmholtz, whose research on acoustics is still standard reading on the subject.

25. HENDERSON CABINET (1825)

Whilst Erard and Haschka were producing multi-pedal effects on their pianos, another fashion found an unlikely home in pianos like this Henderson. The enormous popularity of the Swiss 'musical box' in watches and snuff-boxes was too good an opportunity to lose. So this imposing cabinet piano is, in reality, two instruments in one. In the first place it is a typical cabinet piano of the period, with the usual sticker action (see page 157) producing a clear incisive sound. Then in addition it has a separate set of hammers which are set in motion by a rotating barrel with pricks on it – rather like a giant musical box.

Such instruments were popular in the 1820s, built in such a way that the two instruments could be played together – the performer accompanying the barrel piano, so to speak. One Dr Busby, writing in his memoir *Concert Room Anecdotes* (1825), describes the instrument enthusiastically:

> The time in which it executes any movement may be accelerated or retarded at pleasure; and while by the delicacy and perfection of the mechanism the 'piano' and 'forte' passages are given with correctness and effect, the '*forzandi*' and '*diminuendi*' are produced by the slightest motion of the hand applied to a sliding ball at the side of the instrument.'

When the barrel piano is being played by itself, the action of the hammers is, naturally, upon the damped strings, which gives the instrument its characteristic pizzicato sound. If, however, the dampers are raised, a new 'Pantaleon' effect – like a dulcimer vibrating freely – is brought into play. If the ordinary piano, accompanying the barrel piano, is added, the sonority is remarkably full and satisfying. It is curious that with the undoubted popularity that such instruments enjoyed, there are not many more surviving examples.

The Henderson came into the Collection without a barrel and without the lead weights and gut ropes to turn the clockwork mechanism. Otherwise the piano was in playing order. After a long battle with red tape, the present owner was eventually allowed to import a specially constructed barrel from the workshops of a Spanish craftsman (without having to pay vast sums of duty) and the instrument was put into perfect order. It now has a repertoire of some ten pieces which were popular at the time it was built.

The firm of Clementi and Collard also had great success with instruments of this kind – coincidence or collaboration?

HENDERSON CABINET

Length: 25½″   *Width:* 44¾″
Height of case: 79″
Height: 31″ (floor to keyboard)
Pedals: Two – usual function/side pedal for
   barrel mechanism
Case: Rosewood with brass inlay
Keyboard: Ivory naturals/ebony accidentals
Compass: Six octaves   *Octave size:* 6¼″
Strings: Original   *Wrest pins:* Original
Damping: Cloth   *Bridge:* Divided
Action: Sticker   *Hammer coverings:* Buff leather

26. SCHIEDMAYER SQUARE (*c.* 1827)

Although it is named for Dorner, this piano seems to have been made by Schiedmayer of Stuttgart (see p. 36) since a Schiedmayer in the Germanisches Museum in Nuremberg tallies with this one in almost all respects. The action is what has come to be called 'English', but there the likeness ends. Compared with English actions of the late 1820s, it is refined to a degree never achieved by *our* makers; everything is delicate, as if it has been made by a German or Austrian maker of the later 18th century. The hammer shanks are very slender, and it has the advantage of being one of the first pianos to have the separate adjustable individual flange system for each note; there is also an adjustment to regulate the return of the hammer, so that it does not return to rest too rapidly. Leather hinges for the hammers were beginning to be old-fashioned by this time and there are no traces of them in this instrument. Despite a lack of ironwork, the piano is kept up to modern pitch and holds it well.

The walnut Biedermeier case of this instrument is supported on four doric columns not unlike those of the Haschka Grand (p. 85). Although at first sight the somewhat elephantine legs look unusual, the careful proportions, lack of decoration, carefully-chosen walnut veneers and extreme simplicity soon grow on the onlooker.

The keyboard is typical of early German ones – an octave measuring some six-and-one-eighth inches. It is imposible to see the mechanism of the instrument when it is opened, as the soundboard covers the entire inside of the case. There are two pedals supported on an elegant lyre. The one on the left is a moderator which places a woollen cloth between the hammer and the string, and the one on the right the usual sustaining pedal. The only fault with this system of moderator is that it will not work properly when the sustaining pedal is also being used, because the force of the hammers hitting the moderator cloth tends to sound the string next to the one being struck. This seems to be an insurmountable problem with continental square pianos of the period, which were, of course, diagonally strung. However, when the dampers are lowered, the fault is indiscernible.

This square was bought in Whitstable, Kent in 1955, the then owner having bought it forty years previously in Switzerland. About ten years ago the present owner found its mahogany twin in Vienna, which still had the original leather hammer coverings. Both pianos are now in the Collection.

SCHIEDMAYER SQUARE

Length: 27″ *Width:* 63¾″ *Depth of case:* 10¾″ *Height:* 28″ (floor to keyboard)
Pedals: Two – moderato/sustaining *Case:* Walnut *Legs:* Turned columns
Keyboard: Bone naturals/stained beech accidentals *Compass:* Six octaves
Octave size: 6⅛″ *Strings:* Original *Wrest pins:* Original *Damping:* Plush *Bridge:* Continuous
Action: English with adjustable hammer flanges *Hammer coverings:* Buff leather

27. TISCHNER GRAND (*c.* 1828)

It was at a piano almost identical to this one that the composer Michael Glinka wrote most of his later works. Glinka's piano is preserved in a museum in St Petersburg (Leningrad), and photographs and measurements of it obtained after many months of very diplomatic correspondence finally made it possible to restore this instrument to its original condition.

When the piano first arrived in the Collection it had five French-style tapered and fluted legs, which were quite obviously out of keeping with the rest of the instrument, whereas photographs showed that its Russian sister has four charmingly-designed legs looking rather like elongated Greek vases. Mahogany Georgian bedposts provided the wood in which the latter were copied, and now the Tischner stands proud on authentic legs.

The case is of beautifully figured mahogany, reminiscent in grain of harpsichord-cases, and the lid is of solid mahogany with a simple black ebony line inlaid. The panels of the case are surrounded with crossbanded straight-grained mahogany, also with an ebony line inlaid.

The instrument retains its original lyre and pedals. The pedal on the left works the keyboard shift and the right-side one is divided like the Broadwood pedals prior to 1824, one half acting on the lower dampers and the other on the higher ones. Originally there was a small lever to allow further shifting of the keyboard to give the true *una corda*, but this refinement was removed during a '*ravalement*' which, with great ingenuity, added two extra notes at the top of the keyboard – F sharp and G.

The keyboard has very thick ivory naturals, the usual English-type ebony accidentals, and cornice-type moulding to the fronts of the keys. The design of this moulding, however, is more vigorous than its English counterpart.

The brass knobs for locking the lid of this piano are, fascinatingly, identical with those used by Broadwood in 1821 – clear proof that decorative brassware for furniture was being exported to Russia at the time the instrument was made. There is also a striking resemblance in the nameboard to one on a contemporary Clementi grand piano.

Little is known of the maker, Tischner. He arrived in Russia from Prussia at the beginning of the nineteenth century and soon built himself a fine reputation as a piano manufacturer. Among his more exalted customers, he even numbered the Czar. The firm passed to his son, who was an astronomer, in 1830, but the latter's lack of interest in pianos caused its liquidation soon afterwards.

TISCHNER GRAND

Length: 92½″ *Width:* 48¼″ *Depth of case:* 13¾″ *Height:* 29½″ (floor to keyboard)
Pedals: Two – usual functions (sustaining pedal originally divided) *Case:* Mahogany *Legs:* Four – turned reeded
Keyboard: Ivory naturals/ebony accidentals *Compass:* Six-and-a-half octaves – compass extended later by two notes upwards
Octave size: 6⅝″ *Iron hoops:* One and five iron struts *Strings:* Replaced *Wrest pins:* Replaced *Damping:* Original
Bridge: Divided *Action:* English with adjustable hammer flanges *Hammer coverings:* Buff leather *Recorded:* BBC Archives

28. PAPE SQUARE (1834)

John Field, the artist/composer, is said to have preferred Pape's downstriking square pianos to any others – which seems curious, since the square piano is more associated with the music of Bach's sons than that of the Romantics. However, apart from a certain lack of volume, this instrument fulfils all the requirements of romantic piano music. It is rich and sonorous in tone with an excellent treble, and there is no trace of archaic timbre. Certainly Field found it satisfactory and used it when he played his own piano concertos in Paris.

Johann Heinrich Pape, one of the most versatile and inventive piano manufacturers of the nineteenth century and, with Erard, the most important master working in Paris, was born in Sarstedt near Hanover on 1 July 1789. He came to Paris in 1811 and, after a short visit to England, was won over by Ignaz Pleyel as foreman for his newly-founded piano factory.

A few years later, in 1815, he built his own factory, which he managed with the greatest skill for nearly half a century. Nearly every year he succeeded in making a new invention, or introducing an improvement in the building of pianos. Between 1815 and 1817 he produced one of the first upright pianos after the design of the English 'cottage' pianos. One of his most important innovations was the construction of table-shaped pianos and grand pianos with downstriking mechanisms. Furthermore he introduced the use of felt instead of leather for hammer-heads, cross-stringing, double sound-boards, and a new tuning mechanism – as well as many other improvements. The total number of his inventions, which brought him many high awards, was 137, although only a few of them became generally accepted.

In the fullness of time Pape handed his business over to his son and a nephew. From 1872 to 1885 the firm was managed by 'Mmes Pape et Delouche', but the retirement of its founder signalled the end of the 'Pape' reputation. Heinrich Pape died advanced in years on 2 February 1875 in Asnières, near Paris. As with all Pape's instruments the workmanship of this piano is meticulous to the last degree, and the artistry with which the action is constructed is as superb as that which went into the furbishing of the case.

The unusual '*bois clair*' from which the case is made is in fact birch, with inlays and crossbandings of purple wood and inlaid Greek patterns as well. The birch used is a rare type known as 'weathered birch' – that is, birch that has been struck by lightning or suffered rapid death in some other way, and yet remained standing to be penetrated by rain-water. This water seeping downwards through the tree produces a series of stains in the grain.

PAPE SQUARE

Length: 32½″ *Width:* 72¾″ *Depth of case:* 9¾″ *Height:* 30″ (floor to keyboard)
Pedals: Two – usual functions *Case:* Birch *Legs:* Inverted lyre-shaped *Keyboard:* Ivory naturals/ebony accidentals
Compass: Six-and-a-half octaves *Octave size:* 6⅜″ *Strings:* Original *Wrest pins:* Original *Damping:* Cloth
Bridge: Divided *Action:* Pape's patent downstriking *Hammer coverings:* Buff leather

The six-and-a-half octave compass of the keyboard had by then become normal, and most music of the time could be played within it.

The piano has a brass hitchpin plate, but is otherwise devoid of metalwork. Extra rigidity in the case is the by-product of the downstriking action. All the hammer coverings are original and all retain their virgin coverings of soft felt. Since the action is above the strings, the instrument is almost impossible to tune in the normal way – the piano is basically tri-chord. So there are two levers in the left-hand 'box', which mute the strings to simplify tuning. These are quite definitely not moderators, since there are the usual two pedals to give this effect as well as to sustain (see the Wornum and Wilkinson instrument, p. 58).

When the lid is lifted, a second music rest is revealed on the right-hand side. This, presumably, was for the use of a violinist or flautist.

Pape received a gold medal for this instrument in 1834.

Pleyel grand of 1828 bought in Alsace.

Ignaz Joseph Pleyel was born on 1 June 1757 in Ruppertstal near Vienna. Apart from founding one of the most important French piano-making firms, he also started a publishing business – largely for the publication of his own compositions. The piano factory was founded in 1807, and both this and the publishing house were taken over by Pleyel's son Camille, in collaboration with the composer Friedrich Kalkbrenner (1788-1849) in 1824. Under their management the manufacturing business went from strength to strength, but unfortunately Camille only survived his father by three-and-a-half years, dying on 4 May 1855. His heir to the business was August Wolff, and the firm became known as 'Pleyel, Wolff & Cie'.

A young piano dealer in Lyons who exchanged this upright piano for a small English cabinet piano from the Collection, said he had found it in a junk shop awaiting the removal of its innards and conversion into a cocktail cabinet – a very close call for this exquisite Pleyel!

The exceptionally carefully-chosen flame mahogany veneer matches up from just below the lid, continues onto the keyboard flap, down the front of it and below on the cover above the pedals. The simple legs have lion's paws which are made of composition. A very similar but even more exquisite instrument in Pleyel's own collection is in *bois clair* with purple wood crossbanding. Chopin is supposed to have owned a similar instrument, which is still in Valdemosa, Majorca. Apparently he found Pleyel's pianos the most satisfactory to play and, although they retained the simple English action, he found he could give more expression to his music on them.

The two usual pedals are in brass and the keyboard shift follows Wornum's in shifting to the left (hammers only). The keyboard is in ivory with solid ebony accidentals, and the fronts of the keys are plain polished boxwood without cornices. The keyboard surround is in rosewood, with a simple boxwood nameplate inlaid and the name itself engraved with Indian ink. All the string sizes are marked on the wrest plank, and, in the typical French manner, the string sizes are shown in the middle of the runs – dotted lines being drawn downwards to show where these runs begin and end:

$$\begin{array}{ccccc} & 8 & & 7 & & 6 \\ : \circ & \circ & \circ & \circ & : \circ & \circ & \circ & \circ & : \circ & \circ & \circ & \circ & : \\ : & \circ & \circ & \circ & \circ : & \circ & \circ & \circ & \circ : & \circ & \circ & \circ & \circ : \\ : & & & & : & & & & : & & & & : \\ : & & & & : & & & & : & & & & : \end{array}$$

PLEYEL UPRIGHT PIANINO

Length: 23¼″   *Width:* 44½″   *Height of case:* 43″   *Height:* 28″(floor to keyboard)
Pedals: Two – usual functions   *Case:* Flame mahogany   *Keyboard:* Ivory naturals/ebony accidentals
Compass: Six octaves   *Octave size:* 6½″   *Strings:* Mainly original   *Wrest pins:* Original   *Damping:* Original felt
Bridge: Divided   *Action:* English early upright   *Hammer coverings:* Felt on hollow hammers

The instrument appears to have been re-strung correctly at some time, since the strings have modern eyes. Unlike English and German makers of the time, Pleyel seems to have been a great believer in using thick-covered strings in the bass of his pianos. Indeed, he even went so far as to make a whole piano using single thick-covered strings. This is now in the *Schola Cantorum Basiliensis* Collection in Basel.

The pianino's hammers are of felt on leather throughout, but there is no core as the hammers are hollow – surely a very late revival of Schiedmayer's (or even Cristofori's) early piano features.

The tone and volume of this piano are remarkable and, extraordinarily, the action is far more sensitive than that of a Pleyel grand piano of the same date. It is small wonder that Chopin was so delighted with his 'pianino'.

Grand by Schmidt of Pressburg,
c. 1835. Most 'Viennese' pianos of the
period looked like this. When this piano
was made Pressburg was capital of
Hungary.

30. GRAF GRAND (*c.* 1836)

Conrad Graf was born in 1782 in Riedlingen on the Danube. He studied cabinet-making, arriving in Vienna in 1799 where he was apprenticed to the piano maker, Schelke. In 1804 he opened his own workshop and began a successful career which in 1822 brought him the Freedom of the City of Vienna, and in 1824 the Viennese equivalent of our 'Royal Warrant'. Contemporary reports instance Graf as one of the most distinguished piano-makers in the realm and extol his instruments' ravishingly expressive and romantic tone. Among the better-known users of Graf pianos were Beethoven (for whom Graf made a quadro-chord instrument in 1824 in the hope that it would overcome his deafness), Chopin, Clara Wieck, Schumann and Brahms.

In 1841 Graf sold his business to Carl Stein and went into retirement. He died in Vienna ten years later.

Robert Schumann was given a Graf grand fortepiano as a wedding present in 1839 and the serial number of that piano comes near to this one, which is 2506. Combined with the fact that this one has a label on the soundboard signed by Graf which mentions a Gold Medal he won in 1835, we can date this instrument between 1835 and 1839.

It is a slightly archaic feature of this Graf that the keyboard is 'enclosed', since by 1835 most keyboards were projecting, often with cylinder-shaped covers. The case is exceedingly simple and the

Nameplate of Graf fortepiano, *c.* 1838.

112

GRAF GRAND

Length: 95½"   *Width:* 49¼"
Depth of case: 13"
Height: 27½" (floor to keyboard)
Pedals: Four – keyboard shift/moderato/half
  moderato/sustain
Case: Cherry   *Legs:* Three – turned tapered
Keyboard: Ivory naturals/stained beech
  accidentals
Compass: Six-and-a-half octaves *C₁–g′′′′*
Octave size: 6¼"   *Strings:* Replaced
Wrest pins: Original
Damping: Wedges, thick cloth above
  (*Kastendämpfung*)
Bridge: Divided   *Action:* Viennese
Hammer coverings: Buff leather
Recorded: Argo

turned legs, equally so, are in pleasantly grained cherrywood which has now weathered to a pale apricot colour reminiscent of faded mahogany.

The action is typically Viennese and the stringing tri-chord with the exception of a few covered bi-chord bass strings. These are covered in brass, unlike English covering which was usually in copper. The hammers are covered in brown buckskin as are those of many later Viennese pianos.

The elegant lyre supports four pedals of which the one on the extreme right is the damper-raiser. Next to that is a half-shift moderator, next a full moderator and, on the extreme left, a keyboard shift. Although the instrument is powerful with a clear rich tone, the action is somewhat heavy, as in many late Viennese pianos. Nevertheless the tone more than compensates for this inconvenience, and Schumann rejoiced in his wedding present, being satisfied with it throughout his life.

This Graf came to light in Lucca, Italy, in a poor state of repair. Virtually all of the instrument parts are original, however, even to the wrest pins. It was necessary, though, to replace the hammer coverings which had become as hard as shoe-leather, presumably through water damage.

This Collard and Collard grand, *c.* 1837, still retains a certain classical elegance.

31. WORNUM POCKET GRAND (1837)

Robert Wornum was born in 1780 and died in 1852. There is some mystery about his name, and most suggestions as to its origin seem incorrect. W.L.Sumner, for example, in *The Pianoforte* (Macdonald, 1966) states that it was modified from 'Wornham'. Another authority says that Wornum called himself after the village of Warneham in Dorset. Wornum's own great-grand-nephew avows categorically that Wornum is 'Munrow' spelt backwards.

However he arrived at the name, Robert Wornum went into partnership with Wilkinson in 1810, making pianos in a factory in Oxford Street. This factory was burnt down in 1812 and thereafter Wornum continued making pianos on his own in Store Street, where the Building Centre now stands – not far from Longman and Broderip's late factory in Tottenham Court Road, now Heal's.

At about this time, Wornum produced his small upright piano with diagonal stringing and two pedals – one sustaining and the other for muting one string to facilitate tuning. It was impossible to wedge the strings for this purpose owing to the design of the action.

Wornum was one of the most ingenious English piano builders who virtually invented the modern upright piano action. He never resorted to any form of ironwork in his frames. After the pocket grand Wornum produced a full-sized grand piano – the 'Imperial' grand pianoforte, which was really an enlarged version of his pocket instrument. Constructionally speaking, the Wornum pocket grand is one of the most unusual in the whole Collection. Wornum seems to have started manufacturing this type of instrument in about 1830, and very ingenious it is.

The action rests on the bottom of the case of the piano. On top of this, as an entirely separate entity, hinged onto the lower part of the case, is the stiffly-braced frame complete with strings and soundboard. As the upper part is positioned, the strings are, in effect, *below* the soundboard, and the action, actually a downstriking type, strikes upwards!

To look at, the pocket grand is extremely satisfying – *petite* and at the same time elegant. The case is in plain rosewood which has nevertheless been very carefully selected for graining, and there are two carved brackets, one on either side of the keyboard. The three turned and reeded legs are of solid rosewood, more reminiscent of the late 1820s than of the 1830s; they stand in finely chased brass castors. The simple lyre, quite modern in feeling, holds two pedals. The one on the left is the keyboard shift, but only shifts the top portion of the action supporting the hammers. Since the instrument is bi-chord throughout, this gives an immediate *una corda* effect. The pedal on the right is the sustaining one, but lowers rather than raises the dampers, which are underneath the strings.

WORNUM POCKET GRAND

Length: 66″   *Width:* 45″   *Depth of case:* 14¼″   *Height:* 27½″ (floor to keyboard)
Pedals: Two – usual functions   *Case:* Rosewood   *Legs:* Three – turned reeded   *Keyboard:* Ivory naturals/ebony accidentals
Compass: Six octaves   *Octave size:* 6⅜″   *Strings:* Original   *Wrest pins:* Original   *Damping:* Cloth   *Bridge:* Divided
Action: Wornum's tape check grand   *Hammer coverings:* Felt   *Recorded:* BBC Archives

The ivory keyboard has solid ebony accidentals and the usual English cornice fronts to the naturals. The strings are original as are the wrest pins. These have been bored as was the custom by 1836. The dampers have been re-clothed and the bridges are double-pinned. The action is, for its date, an extremely advanced tape check one, as found in the same maker's piccolo uprights. Compared with almost all other English piano-makers of this date except perhaps Clementi and Collard, Wornum stands alone in having produced the most beautiful and efficient action.

The instrument came to the Collection from the upper room of a Kentish pub from which it was extricated in the 1950s. After some renovation, it was recorded for the BBC Archives by the pianist Malcolm Binns.

Wornum 'piccolo', *c.* 1835. Note the 'early modern' type of action.

Wornum pocket grand of 1836. A 'downstriker' striking upwards.

32. LICHTENTHAL 'DOG-KENNEL' UPRIGHT (1840)

This piano was given to the Collection on one condition: it had to be collected from the previous owner in one week. Luckily, this proved possible – saving it from being used as firewood.

Lichtenthal became well known after he had left his native Belgium for St Petersburg in 1851. Before that time he had been working in Brussels. Most of the instruments that remain with his name on them are of the pianino type and he seems to have specialised in the 'dog-kennel' model, of which this is a perfect example. In spite of the somewhat denigratory nickname which the piano perhaps deserves on design grounds, the 'dog-kennel' fortepiano in fact has a lot to recommend it. It is not too tall, is well made and delicate-sounding. Certainly it must have been popular in the 1830s and 1840s.

Like Wornum and Wilkinson's piano, this one opens up at the side and is also obliquely strung. The action, too, is very like that of the Wornum piccolo piano. The hammers of this instrument are still covered with the original soft felt and there is a metal hitchpin plate. The only pedal is a damper-raiser. The casework is in very pretty mahogany and the inlay and exposed mouldings are in boxwood.

LICHTENTHAL 'DOG-KENNEL' UPRIGHT

Length: 21″   *Width:* 61″   *Height of case:* 40½″   *Height:* 26½″ (floor to keyboard)
Pedals: One – sustain   *Case:* Mahogany   *Keyboard:* Ivory naturals/ebony accidentals   *Compass:* Six octaves   *Octave size:* 6⅜″
Iron hoops: Iron hitchpin plate   *Strings:* Original   *Wrest pins:* Original   *Damping:* Felt
Bridge: Continuous   *Action:* Tape check   *Hammer coverings:* Soft felt

33. PAPE CONSOLE (1840)

The casual observer might well be forgiven for thinking that this tiny piano was in fact a sideboard, for it is only the pedals that give it away. Pape's ingenuity in creating a piano only one-and-a-half inches taller than the height of its keyboard has to be admired, and it is only to be regretted that the complexity of the action means that it does not function quite so well today as it did when it was first produced.

The case in *bois clair* is made of a sort of burr elm. Behind the instrument the fretwork back edge is in reality the cover to the wrest pins. The bracket-type legs make it look much more like a piece of furniture than a musical instrument.

As with Pape's later pianos, the pedals are of beautifully chased brass. They function in the usual way – left for keyboard shift (to the right) and right for raising the dampers.

The keyboard is of ivory with solid ebony accidentals, and extends to some six-and-a-half octaves. There is also extensive metal bracing which makes this deceptively small instrument surprisingly heavy. The original felt hammer coverings are intact, as are the strings, but it has not been possible to bring the piano up to concert pitch and it remains a semitone down.

An identical Pape has been seen in New York, but the majority of his pianos are of rosewood with 'barley-sugar' columns for legs.

Pape console of 1843. A rosewood version with legs more typical than those of the piano illustrated in colour.

PAPE CONSOLE

Length: 20″   *Width:* 52″   *Height of case:* 39½″   *Height:* 30½″ (floor to keyboard)
Pedals: Two – usual functions   *Case:* Burr elm   *Keyboard:* Ivory naturals/ebony accidentals   *Compass:* Six-and-a-half octaves
Octave size: 6⅜″   *Strings:* Original   *Wrest pins:* Original   *Damping:* Original felt
Bridge: Divided   *Action:* Pape's patent   *Hammer coverings:* Original felt

34.   COLLARD AND COLLARD CABINET (1845)

After 1832, the firm of Clementi became Collard and Collard – a welcome simplification of 'Clementi, Collard, Banger, Davis and Collard'.

This magnificent early Victorian piano was bought in 1962 from the music mistress of a Girls' School in Seaford. At that time the case could not have been less fashionable, it would have been considered, by most people, vulgar and overladen. However, on closer inspection, many redeeming features come to light.

The case is of rosewood and the restless decoration in the style of Grinling Gibbons has been executed with care out of solid wood. The designer obviously wished to show his ability to copy past styles *avec grand éclat!* The cornice, however, is exquisitely detailed, and the legs – the strangest part of the woodwork – while weak in design, are also competently worked. Perhaps the most original piece of design in the whole piano is to be found in the beautiful mother-of-pearl inlay around and below the keyboard. This is absolutely 1840-50 Victorian art, on a higher level even than the contemporary 'Berlin' woolwork. Here is no copying of past styles.

Despite a complete lack of ironwork the piano has been successfully tuned up to modern pitch. When it was first bought, it was well below pitch – the bass sounding hollow and gloomy, and the treble like china being broken. Some of the felts in the upper registers needed replacing, but the strings are all original. The tone of the instrument would undoubtedly be improved with complete re-stringing and re-felting, but since the sound is by no means bad, such treatment is really unnecessary.

The action is a very sophisticated type of 'sticker' action. Collard has adapted his grand action for an upright piano and the stickers merely push up to the action, which is situated at the top of the piano.

Clementi, and later Collard and Collard, were famous for their elaborate casework before 1850, but, alas, their names later became associated with an altogether cheaper class of instrument. Collard, particularly, was praised by his contemporaries for his 'little Quaker-like pianos of white wood . . .offered to the public of small means – the needy clerk, the poor teacher, the upper-class mechanic'.

Clementi's early partner, Frederick William Collard, was born in Wiveliscombe, Somerset. He was a prolific inventor and did much to improve the action and construction of pianos. In 1811 he produced a very small upright piano as well as a curious 'square piano' on its side. He died in 1879.

COLLARD CABINET

Length: 26½″   *Width:* 48¾″
Height of case: 73½″
Height: 29½″ (floor to keyboard)
Pedals: Two – usual functions
Case: Rosewood   *Strings:* Original
Wrest pins: Original   *Damping:* Felt
Bridge: Divided
Action: Collard's patent sticker
Hammer coverings: Felt

Lovers of early pianos never know where they are going to come across a new object for their affections. The present owner of this superb Schneider grand fortepiano was leafing through a copy of 'Vogue' magazine in 1960 when he came to a page advertising a dress. The model was leaning against *this* piano. Tracing the piano through the magazine to its owners and bringing it to the Collection was easily managed, but placing it historically less so. It was not until some time later that a good friend, David Kent, found a minute description of the instrument in a catalogue of the Great Exhibition of 1851. Exhibited in the Austrian section by its maker, Schneider, this piano stood in the Crystal Palace. It must have caused quite a stir!

In some respects the instrument is among the last of the classical pianos, and at the same time, among the first of the modern ones. It has a full seven-octave compass, two burnished steel struts and a metal hitchpin plate. The strings with the exception of the covered bass ones are all original, and the action is conventional Viennese, with no adjustments. The pedals are 'soft' and 'sustaining'.

It is the case, however, that is truly exceptional. Exquisitely decorated in bird's-eye maple and wooden mosaic, it stands on three highly ornate legs. The inlay work is very fine, reminiscent of Tunbridge Ware, and the keys, which show almost no overhang at the front edge, are of fine ivory.

The Schneider's hammers share one of the features of late Viennese pianos in that they are felt-covered, but a penultimate layer of leather helps to give the characteristic sweet tone of pianos of this period.

Almost nothing is known of the maker except that he won a medal for progress in Vienna in 1873. Quite a plain piano also by Schneider came to light recently in his native city, but that one was only in walnut. Obviously this ornate instrument was especially designed for the Great Exhibition.

SCHNEIDER GRAND

Length: 95¾″   *Width:* 53½″   *Depth of case:* 14″   *Height:* 28″ (floor to keyboard)
Pedals: Two – usual functions   *Case:* Birdseye maple with wood mosaic inlay   *Legs:* Three – hexagonal tapered
Keyboard: Ivory naturals/ebony accidentals   *Compass:* Seven octaves   *Octave size:* 6½″   *Iron hoops:* Two bars and hitchpin plate
Strings: Original   *Wrest pins:* Original   *Damping:* Leather-covered wedges, cloth pads above   *Bridge:* Divided
Action: Viennese   *Hammer coverings:* Felt with leather outer layer   *Recorded:* Oryx

This is the 'stock' piano of 1850 – many thousands were made in England and France between 1850 and 1880. Liszt had one, so did Wagner and Verdi – but none, surely, as ornately decorated as this. The case is of satinwood, embellished in the style of Louis XVI with three flower inlays on the sides and keyboard fall. On this latter there are also initials which suggest that the instrument at one time belonged to the Rosebery or Rothschild family. The edge of the case is crossbanded in fine amboyna wood with green dyed maple lines. By far the most important of Erard's inventions, still perfect in this model, was the repetition mechanism with 'double escapement' ('*double échappement*') of 1821.

Apart from its striking appearance it is a magnificent piano in its own right and leaves nothing to be desired when played, even though the action is not quite as responsive as a modern Bechstein, Bluthner or Steinway. It is straight strung and has a pressure bar in the treble. All the original strings and felts remain and the instrument is underdamped.

It is curious that with such an impressive reputation there were still those who found Erard's pianos less than satisfactory. Wellcker von Gontershausen writing in 1853 considered that Erard had not made a decent piano until nearly 1820 when his 'perfected action' was used. In fact this point is corroborated by Beethoven who was never satisfied with his 1803 Erard, which was continually being sent back to Streicher for repair and improvement.

A malignant illness ended the full working life of Sebastien Erard on 5 August 1831. It had been a life crowned with success, and ended, curiously, in the same year as that of his great friend and rival piano builder, Ignaz Pleyel. The second generation successors of both Erard and Pleyel, also friendly rivals, both died in 1855.

The second generation Broadwood – James – had died in 1851; Collard was an old man in the 1850s; the early piano manufacturers had provided their beautiful instruments for homes and halls. The firms of Bechstein and Bluthner made their first grands in 1853, Steinway in 1856; beautiful though their sounds were to be, their pianos seldom satisfied the eye as much as the ear – as the pianos in this book surely do.

ERARD GRAND

Length: 101″   *Width:* 52″   *Depth of case:* 13¼″   *Height:* 28¼″ (floor to keyboard)
Pedals: Two – usual functions   *Case:* Satinwood crossbanded in amboyna with ormulu   *Legs:* Three turned and decorated
Keyboard: Ivory naturals/ebony accidentals   *Compass:* Seven octaves   *Octave size:* 6½″   *Iron hoops:* Five bars and hitchpin plate
Strings: Original   *Wrest pins:* Original   *Damping:* Felt underdampers   *Bridge:* Divided
Action: Erard's advanced double escapement   *Hammer coverings:* Felt   *Recorded:* Decca

Part III: The Techniques

1. HOW TO PLAY

These extracts from the *Elementary Instructions* by Hummel, written at Weimar in 1827, should be noted by all who seek to produce the finest sounds from an early piano. Hummel was a piano pupil of Mozart and Clementi.

On Sitting at the Piano-forte

1.   The Pupil must sit opposite to the middle of the key-board, at a distance of from 6 to 10 inches, according to his stature, and the length of his arms; so that the right hand may conveniently reach the highest, and the left hand the lowest keys, without altering the position of the body.

2.   The seat must neither be too high nor too low, and such that both hands may rest on the keys, naturally and without effort. Children should have their feet supported, that their seat may be steady and secure.

On Holding the Body, the Arms, the Hands, and the Fingers

From the outset, particular attention must be directed to these points, since any negligence on this head, drags in its train the most disadvantageous results, such indeed as are scarcely to be amended at a future period; and facility, gracefulness, neatness, expression, and strength of performance will thereby suffer materially.

1.   The *body* must be *held* upright, neither bending forwards nor sideways, and the elbows rather turned, towards the body, yet without pressing against it.

2.   The *muscles* of the arms and hands must act without any stiffness, and with so much force only, as is necessary to move the hands and fingers without languor.

3.   The *hands* must be held in a somewhat rounded position, and turned rather outwards, like the feet, yet freely and without effort; by this means the employment of the thumb on the black keys will be much facilitated. Their position must not be either higher or lower than is necessary to bend the

finger-joints, so as to strike the keys with the middle of the tips of the fingers, and so that the thumb may form a horizontal line with the little finger on the key-board.

Extending the fingers flat on the keys, and, as it were, boring into them, by letting the hands hang downwards are altogether faulty positions, and give rise to a lame and heavy manner of playing.

4. Excepting in extensions, the fingers must neither stand too far apart nor be drawn too close together; each finger should lie naturally over its proper key. They ought not likewise to rest longer on the keys than the prescribed time, as a habit of so doing greatly diminishes the clearness of the performance.

The *thumb* touches lightly the surface of the keys with the edge of its top joint. As it is the shortest of the fingers, the pupil must accustom himself to hold it somewhat bent and inclining towards the first finger, that it may always be ready to pass under the fingers; but it must not be pressed against the other fingers, nor be allowed to drop below the keys.

In general, to attain the necessary facility, steadiness, and certainty in playing, we must avoid every violent movement of the elbows and hands; and the muscles must not be exerted, beyond what a free and quiet position of the hand requires. The quickness of motion lies only in the joints of the fingers, which should move with lightness and freedom, and not be lifted up too high from the keys.

5. The *touch*, or mode of striking the key, must be decisive and equal; all pressure and thumping are to be avoided; neither hands nor fingers should change their naturally bent position; and the keys must be struck rather forwards than backwards on the key-board, that the tone may be more powerful, and the passages delivered with more roundness and finish.

6. Lastly, unbecoming habits should be carefully avoided, as: holding the face too near the book, biting the lips, nodding the head to mark the time, opening or distorting the mouth, &c. &c. as they are prejudicial to the health, and contrary to gracefulness of demeanour.

On the Use of the Pedals

1. A performance with the dampers almost constantly raised, resorted to by way of a cloak to an impure and indistinct method of playing, has become so much the fashion, that many players would no longer be recognised, if they were debarred the use of Pedals.

2. Though a truly great Artist has no occasion for Pedals to work upon his audience by expression and power, yet the use of the damper-pedal, combined occasionally with the piano-pedal (as it is termed), has an agreeable effect in many passages, its employment however is rather to be recommended in slow than in quick movements, and only where the harmony changes at distant intervals: all other Pedals are useless, and of no value either to the performer or to the instrument.

3. Let the Pupil never employ the Pedals before he can play a piece correctly and intelligibly. Indeed, generally speaking, every player should indulge in the use of them with the utmost moderation; for it is an erroneous supposition that a passage, correctly and beautifully executed without pedals, and of which every note is clearly understood, will please the hearer less, than a mere confusion of sounds, arising from a series of notes clashing one against another.

Only ears accustomed to this, can applaud such an abuse; sensible men will no doubt give their sanction to my opinion. Neither Mozart, nor Clementi, required these helps to obtain the highly-deserved reputation of the greatest, and most expressive performers of their day. A demonstration that, without having recourse to such worthless means, a player may arrive at the most honourable rank.

I shall insert here a few cases in which the damper-pedal may be resorted to with the least breach of propriety (p. 133).

On the Touch Proper to Different Piano-fortes of German or English Construction

1. As I have often remarked that the best players are embarrassed by any unusual variation in the mechanism or touch of the instrument – by this I do not merely understand a somewhat shorter and a stiffer touch; for every player should possess thus much power over the instrument – I consider that it will not be amiss to say a few words on this subject.

2. Piano-fortes, generally speaking, are constructed on two different plans, the *German* or *Vienna*, as it is termed, and the *English*; the former is played upon with great facility as to touch, the latter with considerably less ease. Other modes of construction are compounded of these two, or are merely partial variations upon one or other of them.

3.   It cannot be denied but that each of these mechanisms has its peculiar advantages. The German piano may be played upon with ease by the weakest hand. It allows the performer to impart to his execution every possible degree of light and shade, speaks clearly and promptly, has a round fluty tone, which in a large room contrasts well with the accompanying orchestra, and does not impede rapidity of execution by requiring too great an effect. (It is self evident that we speak here only of the instruments of the most celebrated Vienna and German makers.) These instruments are likewise durable, and cost but half the price of the English piano-forte.

4.   To the English construction however, we must not refuse the praises due on the score of its durability and fullness of tone. Nevertheless this instrument does not admit of the same facility of execution as the German; the touch is much heavier, the keys sink much deeper, and, consequently, the return of the hammer upon the repetition of a note, cannot take place so quickly.

Whoever is yet unaccustomed to these instruments, should not by any means allow himself to be discomposed by the deep descent of the keys, nor by the heaviness of the touch; only let him not hurry himself in the time, and let him play all quick passages and runs with the usual lightness of finger; even passages which require to be executed with strength, must, as in the German instruments, be produced by the power of the fingers, and not by the weight of the arms; for as this mechanism is not capable of such numerous modifications as to degree of tone as ours, we gain no louder sound by a heavy blow, than may be produced by the natural strength and elasticity of the fingers.

In the first moment, we are sensible of something unpleasant, because in forte passages in particular, on our German instruments, we press the keys quite down, while here, they must be only touched superficially, as otherwise we could not succeed in executing such runs without excessive effort and double difficulty. As a counterpoise to this, however, through the fullness of tone of the English piano-forte, the melody receives a peculiar charm and harmonious sweetness.

In the mean time, I have observed that, powerfully as these instruments sound in a chamber, they change the nature of their tone in spacious localities; and that they are less distinguishable than ours, when associated with complicated orchestral accompaniments; this, in my opinion, is to be attributed to the thickness and fullness of their tone.

2. HOW TO STRING

This brings up a very thorny question. All things being equal, in replacing a broken string, use exactly the same size as the broken one and loop the eye as nearly as is possible in style to the original one. Even if all three strings on a note are missing, replace them exactly as the ones on either side; if the note is on a transition between two sizes, then take the thinner one. But using another size, even for one string in a note, produces an impure tone, and if all three new strings are equal, but too thin, there will be an unevenness in the tone colour.

However, I have found that the original strings of most early squares speak well, but the strings of many 'transitional' grands from 1818 to 1825 are either too thick for the weakened condition of the piano or have rusted too much to be able to be pulled up 'more or less' to pitch, and give a heavy, thick sound that is unpleasing and certainly not authentic.

Although it is usually best in re-stringing early instruments to use one gauge smaller than the original without loss of tone or volume, in some cases as much as three string sizes smaller actually *improves* both volume and tone and unless the casework 'tension' has absolutely gone, the instruments keep in better tune as well. The 1819 Broadwood grand (p. 70) provides a good example. Since this instrument seemed suddenly to have deteriorated, I reluctantly decided on a re-string. This has been done piecemeal, so that the sound of the new strings could be compared with the old as the re-stringing progresses. First the middle C strings, originally No 12, were replaced by No 9. At once the sound was clearer and brighter and of almost equal volume. It was also far more acceptable. So to the next note, and the next, comparing each with its neighbour so that the tone should be clear and even. The upper register had never been one hundred per cent satisfactory and seemed to be throttled. The thinner strings have cured this fault. (All the old strings are, however, being preserved for reference.)

Each instrument needs its own treatment.

3. HOW TO TUNE

To tune a pianoforte throughout necessitates not only a good ear for 'throbbing' beats: long training and much experience are needed to lay a scale properly and more pianos are injured by amateur (or charlatan) tuners than through any other cause. Hints given here are therefore limited to tuning of unisons and octaves. Owners wanting a complete re-tune should seek a qualified tuner unless or until they have the requisite skills themselves.

A Unison

1.   The knowledge of tuning mostly required by amateurs is that for pulling up a string newly adjusted.

2.   Having put on the string (as already explained) and turned the tuning hammer until the new wire – chipped with a piece of ivory or bone – approximates in pitch to the other strings on the same note, take off the hammer and replace the action.

3.   Readjust the hammer on the tuning pin and with your disengaged hand strike the note. Listening carefully to the sound, turn the hammer very gradually to the right till the quick uneven beats – or sound-throbs – merge into one steady and clear vibration. The string will then be in unison. To make certain that the note will stand, strike it sharply so as to ensure that the string may not slip.

An Octave

1.   If the new string put on is a (single) covered wire in the bass, it must be tuned by the octave note above.

2.   Striking the two notes together, gradually turn the hammer to the right. When the lower note reaches its proper pitch, the uneven beats of the two will cease, and the compound sound produced will blend smoothly.

3.   Care should be taken not to turn the string above its proper pitch or it will break; neither should side-pressure be put on the pin or it may snap off.

4.   Do not turn the pins more than necessary, otherwise they will become loose and the instrument will never stand in tune.

4. HOW TO MAINTAIN

Tuning

A well-restored and basically sound early piano, if properly played on, kept at an even temperature, out of draughts and out of the sun – no fierce central heating, please – will keep well in tune and need comparatively little attention. The owner should at least learn to tune unisons and octaves. Furthermore, when a unison goes out of tune this should be adjusted as soon as possible, thus keeping the instrument in decent sounding order. If the scale wanders, which sometimes happens at the spring and autumn equinoxes, a proper re-tune is essential. An old fashioned T-shaped tuning key is necessary, and this should fit the wrest pins so there is no undue play, otherwise the wrest pins get worn and tuning becomes increasingly difficult. The T-shaped keys are better, as full downward pressure is put on the pins, whereas a modern lever tends to loosen the pin in its socket, although the modern one is easier to use. Old tuners used to suggest that tuning should be carried out with the left or weaker hand, so as not to jerk the strings too quickly, perhaps causing a string to snap.

If one is so fortunate as to possess a grand piano in which the hammers are very accurately centred on the strings the old English method of tuning is as easy as for a harpsichord. The old instructions suggested that one lifted up the *una corda* handstop on the right keyboard block and pressed the left pedal fully down (see Broadwood Instructions p. 73). This shifted the action so that only one string was struck by a hammer per note. This obviated the necessity for a tuning wedge, and also the unpleasant sound of a struck wedged string, which to me makes tuning very difficult. When one set of strings was tuned, the pedal was released, the *una corda* stop lowered, and the pedal pressed down again so the second set of strings could very quickly be brought into unison with the tuned string. Finally the third string was tuned. It would appear that this handstop on most English grand pianos was in fact more of a tuning device than a musical effect. It was used on English pianos until 1843, perhaps even later. When one considers the comparative complication of pulling up this lever, especially when the keyboard shift pedal is down, it really is very impractical to use it as a musical effect during a performance. Beethoven's reference to '*mehr und mehr Saiten*' ('more and more strings') surely assumes the handstop has been already raised, so that one can obtain a crescendo *only*. A diminuendo would be quite impractical.

Tuners

Beware the piano-tuner who looks down on old pianos, better an out-of-tune instrument than the unsympathetic treatment from such a person – broken strings, broken hammers – because the modern way of tuning a piano is to raise the string a shade above the right note and hit the string so hard that the pitch is lowered just that little bit it was raised by in the first place. Such fierce treatment is bad enough for a grand, but can be even more catastrophic with a square, since the leather hinges to the hammers perish with age. Normal playing should do no harm, but banging is as good as murder.

Strings

If an old piano has most of the strings intact, it is a pity to re-string the instrument. Usually if the strings are sound they will pull up to a semi-tone below pitch, with care, after about three tunings. They can be cleaned with emery paper – a ghastly, tiresome job, but well worth it if 90% of the strings still exist.

Old pianos are best kept tuned a semi-tone below modern pitch, since a lower pitch was in use when they were built, and in any case there is then slightly less tension on case and strings. It is surprising how much better an old piano will keep in tune 'a semi-tone down'. Those people wishing to use an early piano in ensembles should have a re-string, using one gauge less than the original, though purists will ask their friends to use gut strings on their violins and tune down to the lower piano pitch. Gut-stringed violins sound far better in consort with old pianos than the modern strung ones. (See p. 136.)

If a string breaks, a string of identical size should be put in. If this is not possible at the time, then at least replace it temporarily with a *thinner* one rather than a thicker one (see p. 136).

Soundboards

English soundboards, because they are usually varnished, will come up like new if cleaned with a damp cloth with a mild detergent. Similarly stiff goose feathers wetted and dipped in mild detergent will clean the dirt from between the wrest pins and under the strings on the wrest plank.

Quite often depressingly large cracks develop in the soundboard, but these defects are best left well alone unless the sound depreciates or rattles develop. There is a brand of 'piano shark' who will try to impress on the layman that cracked soundboards should be removed and repaired or even replaced.

Repairs to English soundboards are comparatively simple on grands, since the bottom boards of the instrument can be removed for attention from *below* the soundboard, as on English harpsichords. Later English grands were fully open at the bottom. Until about 1826 Viennese grands were built like Italian harpsichords, relying on a very stiff base for rigidity, so the bottom cannot be removed; after that the bottoms were open as on English pianos. Cracked soundboards and soundbars that become loose are an insoluble problem, unless the soundboard is removed, repaired and put back again.

Hammers

Till about 1825 on most English pianos, and up till 1860 on most German and Austrian pianos, thick 'buff leather', buckskin, was always used for covering hammers.

Casework

I am very much against stripping and then French polishing old pianos. Very often the old polish will clean with proprietary materials, and if it is necessary to strip and sand down the case, it is usually best to re-polish only partly, and finish off with beeswax and turpentine, allowing at least a year to get the patina to build up, and finally hardening off with spirit. This system is too complicated to describe, but 'old hands' know about it. If the mahogany over-bleaches to an almost white colour, *olive oil* well rubbed in will work wonders. Generally, reasonably faded mahogany looks best on old pianos and it is a pity to try to 'modernize' it. Linseed oil is not very suitable for use on old instruments as it has an unpleasant smell and gets sticky.

Keyboard ivory

Unless ivories are very damaged one can scrape them to remove the stains and scratches. It is best to clean them with a woollen cloth damped down with a mild detergent. In fact keyboards should always be left open during the day – this will cause the ivory gradually to lighten; or, if a rapid bleaching is wanted, remove the keyboard, clean it, and leave it in a sunny window for three or four weeks, which is not a long time compared to the other work necessary in an extensive repair. There is a system of bleaching instruments with ultra-violet light, but although this can be done in two evenings, it gives the keys a deathly white look, not in keeping with the instrument. Proprietary bleaches, peroxide, and lemon juice will not bleach the ivory: all they can do is to remove dirt.

Cloth

The listing tape, which on most old pianos is woollen cloth, can usually be washed in lukewarm soapy or mild detergent water, dried and put back. It is surprising how old flannel comes up when washed, even if quite a lot of colour comes out.

Felt should *never* be used for replacement of cloth. Many people think the cloth is felt, but felt was not used until nearly 1850. Usually flannel, which can be bought at country drapers, is best. It is still even possible to get red flannel, and this should not be cut but torn into lengths and widths as desired. Flannel has a straight edge when torn – and no one can tear felt 'nicely'.

Wrest pins

Wrest pins often get loose after many years' use, especially when pianos have been in centrally heated rooms. The Victorian remedy was to replace them, which is a good idea so long as they are only just an infinitesimal size larger. This idea was abused by buying the standard modern pins which were much larger and boring out the hole larger still, thus wrecking the wrest plank and sowing the seeds of later trouble. If only a few give trouble, an excellent American product called 'Pin-tite', applied sparingly, will within a day or so swell up the wood around the pin. Care must be taken to remove all traces of it as it never quite dries and can cause the end of the string to rust and break. Otherwise one must decrease the hole with a fine veneer to reduce it to its original size.

Loose nut

One of the most tantalising and troublesome faults to diagnose is a partially faulty glueing of the nut. It is almost impossible to see this and much time can be wasted if it is not discovered. The chief symptom is a 'short' sounding note with almost no sustaining power. The difficulty is to *see* what is awry, because the old dirt accumulates near the nut, and what is often a crack is not observed. An easy test for the trouble is to press the hammer part of the tuning key as near to the guide pins as possible, on the nut, press very hard and strike the note. Try this again without pressure – and one does not have to be an expert to hear the difference in the sound. Exactly the same thing applies to the bridge.

Dampers

The 'converted harpsichord jack' dampers of English pianos are generally not too efficient, but Kalkbrenner preferred the vague damping of English pianos to the precise 'dry' Viennese type. These often have been renewed with modern damper felt, which will not work sympathetically. It is better to remake them with white flannel as mentioned above. Very early English squares use a sort of sandwich of several layers of buff leather for the damping material; this is also sometimes used under the keys instead of box-cloth. Those early squares with overdampers and whalebone springs to add pressure to the damping often suffer from broken whalebone springs. These cannot be obtained any more since whales, thank goodness, are protected animals. The best substitute is black celluloid. (Whalebone from old corsets has usually become so brittle that it is alas almost impossible to re-utilise.)

Damping on Viennese pianos was particularly good since they utilised wedge dampers at a very early date, 1770 or so. These were arranged so that little triangular wedges of wood were covered in wash-leather. From slightly above middle C, where stringing was often trichord, just plain thick soft buff leather was used, with no wedges.

Glues

All repairs to old pianos should be made with a water-soluble glue or one that can be re-melted with a *chemical solvent*. Many repairs, particularly to soundboards, have been done in the past with epoxy glues that cannot be 'undone', so that second repairs are almost impossible to effect and more damage is done to remove the soundboard than was in the first place necessary to repair. A soundboard once glued in with epoxy is there for keeps, but it is sometimes necessary after a few years to remove a soundboard again – things do go wrong even with repaired pianos. Water-soluble glues are the best and easiest to work with – old-fashioned fish glue is after all how the piano was put together in the first place. Gentle steaming and so forth will undo old work easily and fairly quickly, and soundboards can be readily removed overnight, with damp cloth placed in the requisite position.

Professional restorers and repairers

There are now quite a number of reputable people who will restore old pianos, but their prices are very high. This is not a rapacious racket: full-scale restoration is a delicate and time-consuming job demanding care and patience as well as expert knowledge and experience. It is best to discuss the instrument carefully with the restorer so you know what you are getting. A professional restorer will be pleased to explain what you want to know, but beware the inexperienced amateur who offers to do the job cheaply for you.

5. HOW TO DATE

Few people would be likely to buy an old piano without having some vague idea when it was made, but most would probably want to know exactly when it left the maker's workshop. This can be very difficult to find out, since few records now exist. Erard, for example, who had a large English factory, had their historical books thrown away in the 1920s. However, a great many of the Broadwood books, which were thought to have perished in the 1941 wartime bombing, were later found by Stuart Broadwood in the stables at Lyne, and these give helpful information.

The obvious first approach to the age of a piano is through the casework, but this is not always conclusive, and there are many subtle details to notice in dating old pianos. Any summary of the mechanism or design used at a particular period can only point to an approximate date, since in all historical designs there is always a first example, sometimes many years in advance of the average, and certain details also linger on for a time after the general trend has become obsolete. The following notes on dating should therefore be taken only as a general guide.

The notes tend to concentrate on Broadwoods, not only because they are well documented but because by 1810 Broadwoods had the largest piano factory in the world; their instruments so far outnumbered those of all other English and Continental builders – even the large organisations like Stodart, Clementi, Tomkison and Erard – as to be almost a monopoly.

Series Numbers

Generally speaking, all pianos were numbered, and Broadwoods can give a date today for theirs if the number is known. They numbered each type of piano separately, that is to say grand pianos had one series, squares another, and so on. Various numbers appear on different parts of the instrument, but the main series number was placed in a conspicuous position, in ink – usually on the left-hand side of the wrest plank near the last bass string, very often with the date on the right-hand side of the wrest plank above the top treble string. This arrangement was adopted in 1810 when the custom of dating pianos on the nameboard was discontinued. The number was repeated in different places, so that if the ink number has been rubbed off through cleaning, there are likely to be others stamped on.

Tomkison always stamped the number with his name on the wrest plank on grands, and in the left-hand 'box' on squares. Clementi, and later Collard and Collard, had an ink number on the wrest plank, or near the wrest pins on a square, and stamped numbers were only factory identification numbers. This is very important, as many people take the stamped numbers as piano series numbers.

Dates and Numbers on Squares

Many squares of up to 1836 or later had their dates written in ink or pencil on the bottom key, and occasionally, too, on the last key, written either on top of the key lever, or on the side where it is invisible until the key is removed. On some squares the date and keyboard maker's name occur on the actual keyboard frame, either in the bass or treble *under* the keys, so that only when the action is removed and the keys taken out is this little piece of information visible.

The number is always put on the inside of the dust covers, which are usually green or white.

Dates and Numbers on Grands

On early grands the dates and numbers occur in the most curious places. Dates are not so frequent, but the numbers occur as follows:

> In chalk on the under side of the lid and on the music rest
> On the trestle stand on the upper front cross member between the pedals
> Under the pedal(s)
> On the edge of the loose front board (grands)
> On the back of the nameboard
> On the damper ruler (grands)
> On the keyboard blocks and sometimes on the back of the *una corda* handstop
> On the action
> On the top or bottom keys
> On the keyboard frame under the keys
> On the keyboard flap cover on later grands
> On turned legs at the top next to the wooden thread (also sometimes dated)
> On the tenon of the cross member of a trestle stand
> On the actual case of the piano
> On the top or bottom jack type damper (occasionally, on very early grands).

Wornum usually dated his pianos on both the bottom and the top key, giving the dates of 'conception' and 'birth' so to speak – usually involving a 'gestation' period of six months.

Nameboards and Inscriptions

Broadwood inscriptions continued to be in Latin until 1793, but from 1794 when John Broadwood took his son into the business, the English nameplate was contained in an oval *etiquette* inlaid into a satinwood fascia board. Until 1794 Broadwood fascias were sycamore. Tomkison used sycamore until about 1810.

The oval name and satinwood nameboard persisted after the 'new six-octave' instruments were made, until 1813; then the nameboards were usually of rosewood with an oblong 'printed' nameplate. But instances of satinwood nameboards continued on squares until 1825. By 1814, however, the choice of casework began to diversify. For a very short period – *c*. 1825-27 – Broadwood's nameboard on grands was made the same height as the keyboard cheeks and did not divide up the fascia.

Fretwork was usually adopted on the nameboard about 1795 when the compass was extended upward to c''''.

Flower paintings incorporated with the name on the nameboard were in vogue from about 1796 to 1807, though some makers had dainty little painted *etiquettes* till the mid 1820s. (For the flowers depicted on a typical 1805 instrument see the list on p. 92).

By 1820 the fretwork was superseded by a much simpler diagonal grille, and in 1824 this was usually replaced by a similar design in pierced brass. After that there was a reversion to the wooden fretwork, but mostly coarser and more florid in design, rather lacking in restraint.

In 1800 Broadwoods received the Royal Warrant so, except for the odd rarity as described below, instruments bearing the words 'Makers to His Majesty and the Princesses' must be after 1800; those without them, before. Broadwood's inscriptions can be puzzling, however, since some pianos have a slightly different 'Royal Warrant' wording. Most instruments refer to 'Makers to *His* Majesty etc.' after 1800 when Broadwood received the Royal Warrant, and very few to 'Makers to *Their* Majesties'. This can be explained as follows:

Period	*Inscription*
From 1800 until 1820	His Majesty (George III alone)
1820 till 1821	Their Majesties (George IV and Caroline)
1822 till 1830	His Majesty (Caroline died in 1821)
1830 till 1837	Their Majesties (William IV and Adelaide)

Broadwood nameboards of 1793, 1794 and 1819.

In 1808 a second Broadwood son was taken into partnership, so that when the name appears as 'John Broadwood and Sons' the instrument is almost certainly after 1808. However this detail does not invariably clinch the date of making. Broadwoods also repaired and 'did up' pianos, sometimes for the owners and sometimes following a 'trade-in' which they exchanged in part sale of a more modern piano. The instrument taken back, if good enough, was repaired, done up, modernised, and resold – with a new nameboard. Thus quite a number of older pianos which still bear their original series number had the nameboard either replaced or altered later on. Broadwoods would supply new nameplates to owners of their pianos only on condition that the old one was sent back to them.

Compass

The earliest English grands had a simple five-octave compass, $F,$-f''' and this was usual until about 1792. But in 1796 Broadwoods made one of six octaves, $C,$-c'''', for Don Manuel Godoy. It seems that in that year an additional half octave to c'''' was added to the treble of most of their five-octave pianos. Those 'extra notes' are observed under the soundboard on squares, and are called for especially in much music of the late eighteenth century.

Very recently other six-octave Broadwood pianos have come to light, as early as 1808, showing that the company did not stop making five-and-half octave instruments until about 1810. Something like 5,000 six-octave instruments were being made till 1822 or 1823, still without iron bars.

In 1810 Broadwood extended the compass of all pianos further downard to $C,$ and this persisted generally till just after 1821. No wonder that when Wornum, in 1830, produced an upright of six octaves $F,$-f'''' only three feet to four-and-a-half feet high, this was the beginning of the end of squares. Shortly after this a six-and-a-half octave compass was produced, and gradually the compass was increased both upwards and downwards until by 1850 a full seven-octave instrument was complete.

Keys

English makers used ivory for the naturals and ebony for the accidentals, and the fronts of the keys were finished with a varnished beech moulding. Later on, about 1845, a simple flat sliver of varnished maple sometimes replaced the moulding. By the time of the Great Exhibition in 1851 all this changed: the key fronts also were of ivory, and by then the seven-octave 'modern' piano was the rule.

Hammer Coverings

Hammer coverings, if the actions have not been altered, can help to fix dates. All early pianos without exception had their hammers covered with buckskin or wash-leather. This system went on until about 1825, when cloth and then felt began to be used. Shortly after 1820, particularly on squares, the bass part of the piano – i.e. those notes on the bass bridge – had cloth-covered hammers. Gradually the cloth or felt was extended, until by about 1839 only the topmost octave was covered with leather.

Stringing

It is often difficult to know for sure if an instrument has been re-strung, because up till 1850 it was done by the same methods as originally. But many later amateur repairs and replacements are easy to see, since the new strings were usually too thick or too thin, and the symmetrical pattern of the stringing was spoilt.

After 1819 bi-chord close-covered strings were used for the last few bass notes (about five) instead of three single plain strings.

It seems that Broadwoods used individual strings, each with a proper loop for the eye, until about 1850. After that they adopted the then more modern idea of passing a string round a large hitchpin and joining it up to another wrest pin without any eye. Collard and Clementi, though, used this system in about 1827 when it was patented by Stewart. Erard used *agraffes* as early as 1808, but Broadwoods did not adopt this system until much later, and not until 1850 did they use a pressure bar. 'Screw-in' wrest pins were patented by Broadwoods in 1862.

Iron Tension Bars (Hoops)

Broadwoods have claimed that they used iron tension bars as early as 1808 and that from three to five bars were used in grands of 1821. The first metal hitchpin plate was used on squares in 1821, and a combination of metal bars and metal hitchpin plate was in use on grands by 1827. But this was only on prototypes; these devices were not in general use until later.

Types of Action

Longman and Broderip used an adjustable hopper action after 1786, but with mopstick overhead dampers. By separating the function of the action and dampers, each part could be regulated individually and the damping adjusted without upsetting the touch. By 1810, for certain, all Broadwood squares had hopper and escapement actions. In 1826 one could opt for a hammer check as mentioned above. No other changes in the actions of Broadwood's squares have been observed, until 1836, when the hammers were hinged as in a grand, with a wire through the axis, instead of parchment. Nonetheless Zumpe used this system on the dampers in 1766.

Broadwood's 'new model' squares of 1784 had a very ingenious method of underdamping the strings, with beautifully made brasswork levers, activated by another leather button just below the leather 'old man's head' which activated the hammer. It is however still a 'single' action, and was not altogether ideal as the touch was difficult to regulate. This system continued until at least 1805.

Damping Systems

The damping system of early English pianos was a conversion of the harpsichord jack into a damper. A 'square piano' damping system with bigger 'dolly' dampers was evolved after 1805. Some time after 1850, for a period, Broadwood used *under*dampers on grands, a system Erard used from 1821.

From the earliest years until about 1810 the whole compass of five or five-and-a-half octaves was damped; and the six-octave instruments of 1810-13 were also wholly damped. By 1815 the top half octave was no longer damped, though the instrument retained damper shafts with no damper material, to avoid a change in weight of touch. After 1818, instead of these dummy dampers the keys of the top octave were weighted with lead to balance the touch. Shortly after 1815 the penultimate octave had considerably lighter cloth for damping, obviously to reduce the difference between damped and undamped strings in the treble. The top dampers were a curious mixture of 'harpsichord jack' and square piano 'dolly' dampers, on a wire extension.

To summarise:

Until 1813: the whole piano was damped with 'converted' harpsichord jacks
1814-18: dampers on five octaves, top half-octave dummies
1818-24: last notes undamped; composite dampers on penultimate half-octave
1824-32: five octaves only damped
c. 1833 onwards: 'modern type' dampers.

There are numerous other little details which can help to date an early Broadwood grand.

Up till about 1805 the hitchpin rail had a small moulding at the outer edge. It seems no cloth was used between the moulded edge and the hitchpins, and the unused part of the strings was damped by a woven *silk* braid threaded through. After 1805 a strip of woven cloth was placed immediately in front of the hitchpins under the eye of the string, over which ran the strings, damping the unused part. From 1805 until about 1810 a small fillet of wood covered with woollen cloth was placed between the nut and the wrest pins to damp the unused part of the strings. Before and after those dates silk braid, and afterwards listing tape, often canary coloured with a pattern woven into it, was threaded through.

Pedals

By 1806 the pedal mechanism was hidden by a simple fretwork-style lyre. At the same time a third pedal was added – or rather the sustaining pedal was divided. It is difficult to say when this system was dropped. In 1810, when trestle stands were dispensed with in favour of turned legs screwed directly into the casework of the piano, a screw-on lyre was adopted. On elegant pianos the legs were often elaborately inlaid, reeded, and carved, with brass ferrules near the top. Instances with a divided pedal exist as late as 1824.

Casework

Generally speaking, from the 1780s the earliest Broadwood grands had plain mahogany cases with crossbanded edges to the case, with a white line of box or sycamore. The sides were carefully chosen veneer, the top lid usually solid mahogany with no crossbanding, but a boxwood line inlay. The legs were plain 'Chippendale' type, and the pedals protruded inwards from the legs. The nameboard was of sycamore with the name inscribed in Latin. Furthermore the bridge was in one continuous piece like that of a harpsichord up till 1788.

The earliest Broadwood grands had a slightly more elaborate moulding along the bottom of the case. This was continued until 1793, after which a simple quarter-inch round concave fillet sufficed.

In 1806 the boxwood line dividing up the inlaid panels was replaced by an ebony line as a sort of mourning gesture to Nelson who died at Trafalgar in 1805; this detail persisted on plain pianos until 1824. More elaborate grands with rosewood crossbanding were being made from 1810 onwards, so in these cases the black line was not used.

By 1830 the practice of dividing the lid and sides into panels either by crossbanding or inlay was abandoned in favour of more elaborately grained wood, with the grain on the sides laid vertically instead of horizontally.

The earliest Broadwood pianos had delicate drop handles. On more elegant instruments the handles were chased and gilt. When Broadwood produced his new six-octave grand in 1810, he replaced the drop-handles with classical-shaped brass or brass gilt handles.

Base Boards

A point well worth remembering is that all early grands until 1821 had closed-in base boards. After this, the bottom board was replaced by a light frame covered with canvas. Often these frames are missing.

Legs and Stands

The legs are a good indication of the date of a piano. The earliest squares and grands invariably had trestle stands (as illustrated), but quite early on more elegant squares would rest on a 'French' stand: Ganer squares as early as 1778, and a Broadwood square by 1787. These 'French' stands consisted of four elegant tapered legs which could be taken apart for easy transport. Square tapered legs were used on 'elegant' grands from 1780 till turned legs were adopted about 1810. Plain Chippendale legs (untapered) were available until about 1804, when tapered legs were generally adopted.

Another small point that helps to date Broadwoods' grands after 1810 is that there were four turned legs, two in the front and two about two feet from the tail. This system continued until about 1830, when only one back leg was retained at the tail. Other English makers, however, sometimes used three legs much earlier.

The choice of casework can, however, mislead one as to date, since an instrument of 1780 by Merlin might have tapered legs and satinwood crossbandings just like those of a Broadwood of 1805. Such an instrument would have to be dated by its number or other minor details.

Music Rests and Candlestick Stands

The earliest music rests were very elaborate affairs. From about 1780 they were designed to slip into the instrument above the wrest pins. They slid backwards and forwards and had several refinements of adjustment, for the ease of the player. They could be tilted forward or back and the angle could be locked in position by a small bolt. The central tilting part could be raised or lowered and again locked in position at the most convenient height. These devices nearly always had the piano series number stamped on underneath. At each side was a forward-sliding platform for a candlestick so that the candle would illuminate the music. In the earliest of these the candle stood on fretwork, rather as on the earlier harpsichord. By 1800 this was replaced on Broadwoods by a plain piece of mahogany, in 1804 by a simple fretwork cross, and by about 1818 by a plain mahogany shelf once again.

There were many variations on this theme, however, and some makers gave their pianos very elaborate candle-holders. It is a little risky to try and date a piano solely by its music rest or candlestick stand. By 1830 Broadwoods had abandoned the height adjustment on their music rests, and by 1900 even the candlestick stands were fixed.

Keyboard Covers

By 1827 when both metal hitchpin plates and iron tension bars were used, the keyboard protruded forward from the case and was not enclosed as in earlier instruments. A keyboard cover, not unlike those on modern instruments, was evolved, called a cylinder front on account of its cylindrical shape which made the pianos look shorter than earlier ones with enclosed keyboards.

Variety of Choice

We have seen how cheaper pianos retained older details and the more expensive and elaborate ones had the very latest inventions and detailing. Broadwood made 7,000 square pianos and 1,000 grand pianos between 1782 and 1802, and something like 150,000 of all pianos up to 1850, and there seemed to be no end of variations on a basic design. Square pianos in particular lent themselves to unbelievable variety by the end of the second decade of the nineteenth century, after the Napoleonic wars, when the bourgeoisie of England had become wealthy enough to afford pianos; many mutations could be effected – thus adding enormously to the difficulty of dating.

Let us take a simple example of a square of 1820. Basically it would be of mahogany, with six mahogany turned legs which had certain parts ebonised, with brass castors, and a simple inlaid line on the lid and the case; it would have one pedal, and five-and-a-half octaves. But one could ring the changes as follows, and if desired incorporate in the same piano one or all of the following features – each dating originally from a different period:

Two music drawers between the outer legs

A third drawer between the centre legs

More elaborate inlays

Different woods, e.g. mahogany with rosewood crossbanding, later on all-rosewood with brass inlays, or rosewood with satinwood crossbanding

Elaborately reeded legs with brass ferrule tops; these could be further elaborated by the reeds being made to go round and downwards in a twist

An extra half-octave making six octaves

The extended compass could be used either upwards or downwards making $F, -f''''$ or $C, -c''''$

The corners could be rounded.

A few years later one could have the added luxury of a metal hitchpin plate, and by 1826 a more sophisticated check action. In fact squares with this refinement are about the only ones that can really be adjusted satisfactorily and played properly, almost as a modern piano. Alas there is only a miniscule period from which one can have a square that plays perfectly and looks very elegant. Now that fashion accepts turned legs and even fairly coarse Victorian detail, square pianos up to 1855 or so make good musical instruments, but the sound is beginning to get 'modern'.

TECHNICAL TERMS

These definitions and explanations relate to the classical pianos in this book. Modern practice incorporates many so-called improvements.

Action: The mechanism whereby the player, by pressing a key, sets the hammers in motion so that they strike the strings either loudly or softly or at any intermediate variation between ff and pp. (See also 'Downstriking Action' and 'Viennese Action'.)

Balance Rail: A rail on the keyboard frame on which the keys are pivoted and the keys balanced. Without it the keys would not move evenly.

Bridge: A wooden moulding glued onto the soundboard, and pinned in such a way that the strings pass over from the wrest pins to the nut and to the bridge and beyond to the hitchpins. The portion of the strings between the nut and the bridge is the only part that is used for the propagation of sound. The part of the string between the bridge and the hitchpins is usually damped with woollen cloth to stop unnecessary vibrations, which would upset the true functioning of the instrument.

Check: Usually a leather-covered strut, the top of which forms a pad to catch the hammer on its return from striking the string and so stop it from bouncing back against the string and causing an unpleasant jarring sound. On well-adjusted actions, immediately the key is released the player can strike the string again (see 'Repetition').

Covered Strings: The heavy bass strings consisting of a copper or iron core onto which a thinner copper string is spun to create a thicker string and thus give more sonority. This has been overdone in very small pianos, but it is surprising what good sonority can be obtained with comparatively short covered strings.

Damper: A device to stop the strings vibrating. When a key is depressed the damper is raised, removing the device so that the strings vibrate freely. Dampers vary much in early pianos, but the principle is always the same. In old pianos, the damping material usually consists of layers of woollen cloth. In Continental instruments it is often soft leather, forming wedge-shaped devices in the lower octaves, and plain soft leather in the higher octaves. Only 'modern' pianos after about 1840 had felt for the dampers.

Downstriking Action: The great majority of horizontal pianos have their actions below the strings, so that the hammers strike upwards against the strings, which tends to move the string away from the bridge. This has certain disadvantages, and several makers decided to try and overcome these by designing pianos with the action *above* the strings so that the hammers struck downward onto the strings. Schröter in the eighteenth century tried this, so did Streicher in Vienna, Pape in France, and Wornum in England. It may not be generally realised that all uprights except the early upright grands do in fact use the downstriking system – that is, the hammers strike the strings towards the bridge and soundboard and not away from it as in a grand.

Escapement: When a hammer is put into motion by the key via the action via the jack, it has to be stopped from jamming against the string after it has struck it. Therefore, after the jack has met the hammer butt, it is allowed to 'escape' so that the hammer can fall back immediately it has attacked the string. This is the whole essence of pianoforte action.

Genouillère: A device, usually directly under the keyboard, serving the same purpose as a pedal. *Genouillères* were made of wood, flat shaped, and were activated, as the French word indicates, with the knee, lifting the device by raising the heel the (opposite of a foot pedal which is operated by the toe). They were much tidier looking than foot-operated 'pedals', which were usually suspended on a lyre-shaped frame. Some Continental pianos had as many as five *genouillères*. On English instruments, particularly squares, the *genouillère* was also used for raising the small lid flap on the right-hand side of the keyboard to act as a 'swell'. There were often combinations of *genouillères* and pedals.

Guide Pins: Pins placed on the bridge and nut to keep the strings in a permanent position so that the hammers strike the strings always in the same place.

Hammer: A device covered with soft leather – in fact a hammer – that strikes the strings to produce the piano sound. Only at a later date were hammers made of felt.

Hammer Butt: A notched piece of wood to which the end of the hammer shank is attached, to enable the action of the piano to bring the hammer into attack. The notch enables the 'hopper' to escape so the hammer does not jam against the strings (see 'Escapement').

Hitchpin: A metal pin, usually brass in classical instruments, over which the string is looped.

Hitchpin Block or Rail: A wooden block into which all the hitchpins are driven – in grands it is a hitchpin rail, which follows the curve of the instrument.

Hopper: A piece attached to the back part of a key to raise the hammer and regulate the distance to which it falls back from the string after striking it.

Irish Dampers: An interesting system that simplified the damping of early squares and at the same time saved space. It utilised a 'dolly' type of damper attached directly to the end of the key instead of to an intermediate set of hinged levers. However, it had two great disadvantages: first, in order to remove the action for any minor repairs or adjust-

ments, all the dampers – at least 55 – had to be unscrewed; and secondly the sustaining pedal, when operated, lowered the keys slightly, so that the attack was altered.

Jack: In a piano action there is a jack which has a quite different function from that of the jack in a harpsichord. Rosamond Harding describes it as 'A fixed upright on the key serving to communicate motion from the key to the hammer.' The word 'fixed' here is slightly misleading: it is fixed in the same way as the hammer is fixed, but on early pianos it is hinged.

Kapsel: A German term used for a brass U-shaped 'axle-box' or bearing into which the hammer-shank in German (Viennese) pianos is pivoted at about nine-tenths of its length, so that the extension of the hammer can swivel and attack the keys (see *Prellmechanik*).

Key: The device (usually ivory-covered) which serves to set the hammer in motion (via the action and the jack).

Keyboard: The whole range of the keys. The early keyboards on harpsichords had a compass even smaller than four octaves, whereas Bösendorfer now make an eight-octave piano.

Key frame: A wooden frame which carries the keys and action. Germans call the frame descriptively *Schlitte* (sledge) because it really does slide in and out of the instrument.

Moderator: A strip of woollen cloth on a thin batten which by means of a pedal (or *genouillère*) is inserted between the hammer and the strings to produce a softer, slightly reedy sound. Mainly used on Continental pianos; latterly cheap English pianos have employed this system, but used soft felt instead.

Mopstick: The old-fashioned term for the type of damper used on the earliest square pianos. They were wooden levers hinged with parchment to the back of the instrument; the damping cloth placed at the front of the lever gave the impression of an old-fashioned mop in miniature.

Nut: A pinned wooden moulding on the wrest plank over which the strings pass. Beyond the nut is the important vibrating part of the string.

Old Man's Head: The leather-covered knob on early square pianos which raises the hammer in order to strike the string. No doubt it was reminiscent of a man's bald head.

Open-covered Strings: A type of covered string used on very early square pianos. Instead of the copper outer string being closely wound, each turn of the spiral was spaced at about one thirty-second of an inch from the next.

Overstringing: A system which applies only to modern pianos. It consists of taking the bass strings over and across the middle section of the piano, to obtain extra length in the bass strings. It would not have been possible to achieve this on early instruments with very slender tapered cases.

Pedals: Devices suspended from a lyre-shaped frame and worked by the feet to activate certain mechanical parts which effect a modification of sound. Some Continental pianos had as many as seven pedals. The usual system, even in the period covered by this book, had two pedals only, the one on the left to shift the keyboard to the right, the one on the right to raise the dampers.

Prellmechanik: A German term for which the nearest translation would be 'flick-mechanism'. It simply describes the early German (Viennese) piano action. The difference between this and the *Stossmechanik* is very important. In the *Prellmechanik* the hammer shank has an extension or 'beak' beyond the fulcrum which, when the key is depressed, catches on a projection (*Preller*), so giving the shank a 'flick' which

causes the hammer to jump up towards the string to strike a note. The hammer is pivoted so that it is nearer the keyboard than the shank to which it is attached.

Ravalement: The word used by French piano and harpsichord makers for a major overhaul, often including an extension of the compass.

Repetition: The means of repeating a note. Although the repetition was excellent on early pianos (in spite of the modern misunderstanding that old pianos had poor repetition), it was more *difficult to achieve* than on modern pianos. The finger had to be lifted right off the key before one could repeat a note. This meant that the player had to have very nimble fingers, whereas with a modern action one hardly needs to raise the finger from the key to get immediate repetition.

Ruler: A 'left-over' from the harpsichord, this is a wooden moulding, the underside of which is covered with soft cloth, stretching across the strings above the dampers to stop them from jumping out of the piano.

Soundboard or Belly: A thin deal board onto which the bridge is fixed and over which the strings are stretched. It amplifies the sound of the vibrating strings; without it only a thin sound would result.

Sticker Action: A method of using rods or 'stickers' to transmit motion between the ends of two reciprocating levers, first used in organs, then on cabinet pianos, and later on cottage pianos and cheaper upright pianos to connect the escapement to the hammer.

Stickers: Wooden rods (rectangular) used in the Sticker type of action to transmit motion from the keyboard to the hammers two to three feet higher at the top of the piano, the hoppers being used at the end of the keyboard.

Stossmechanik: A German term for which the nearest translation would be 'push-mechanism'. It describes the English system of piano action by which the hammer is brought into motion simply by a rod or stick which lifts it by giving it a push at the butt. The hammer faces in the opposite direction to the German actions (see *Prellmechanik*), with the hammer butt nearest to the player. All modern actions use a much more advanced technique, but the principle is the same.

Strings: The metal wires which vibrate when struck by the hammers. They were usually made of brass in the lower octaves and soft iron in the treble.

Swell: This device does not really apply to pianos. It was first used on organs. Shudi adapted this for harpsichords, as a means of getting 'expression' into a harpsichord to compete with the expressive piano. A 'swell' is basically a device by which one can open or close an instrument to let out more sound or to deaden the sound. The early ones were like Venetian blinds placed above the soundboard that could be opened or closed by pedal or *genouillère* (see *genouillère*). Very few pianos exist with this device.

Tuning Fork: A small metal device which when struck will always resonate with a fixed note, usually G, A, or C, from which one can judge the pitch of the piano and thence tune it correctly.

Tuning Key: A device, usually T-shaped, that fits over the wrest pins and by which they are turned to adjust the tension of the strings for tuning. Modern tuning keys are like a kind of motor-car spanner.

Una Corda: Literally 'one string'. On tri-chord pianos when the little handstop on the right keyboard block is raised it allows the 'soft' pedal when depressed to shift the action across the strings so that only one string per note is struck. This device was also used for tuning the instrument. It is nowadays simply an instruction to use the soft pedal.

Viennese Action: The Viennese or German action was a very important rival to that on the English type of piano. Most of the major Continental composers were brought up on and were familiar with this type of action, and they used it and preferred it to the English action until about 1840. Erard's 1821 action, English in conception, was however so responsive that the Viennese and earlier English types slowly lost ground. Yet the Viennese type still persisted until about 1910. Its advantages were simplicity of construction, very light touch, remarkable facility of repetition, and little need for continual adjustment.

Wrest Pin: A hardened thick iron nail which has its top flattened out to take the tuning key or tuning hammer. The string is wound around it in such a way that the wrest pin can be turned and the tension of the string thus varied to alter the pitch, so as to 'tune' the string to its required note. Early instruments relied on a clever method of wrapping the string round the pin without the need of the hole through which the string passes in modern pianos. The old soft iron wire was easy to wind around in this way: with modern wire it is almost impossible.

Wrest Plank: A wooden block with holes bored to take the wrest pins, which enable the strings to be stretched to produce a musical sound.

ACKNOWLEDGEMENTS

This book has been in gestation for about thirty years. Many old friends who gave me help and information have now passed on, alas, but nevertheless I wish to record my thanks to them. I have not given a bibliography as it would be too large and many books are based on only superficial knowledge and are therefore not worth mentioning. Five, however, are of particular value:

C.Montal, *l'Art d'accorder soi-même son piano*
Rosamond E.M.Harding, *The Piano-Forte*
Franz Josef Hirt, *Meisterwerke des Klavierbaus*
Heinrich Welcker von Gontershausen, *Der Flügel*
Edward F.Rimbault, Ll.D., *The Pianoforte – its Origins, Progress, and Construction* 1860.

My thanks and appreciation are given to many people, some who perhaps even gave me only a morsel of information or encouragement, but everyone has helped whom I mention, and particularly John Broadwood and Sons who let me have access to their historical papers, which has made the task of writing this book much easier.

First of all, my wife for being very patient with me and helping me sort out remote details from my archives.

Isolde Ahlgrimm; Aldeburgh Festival Society; Lady Aldington; Lady Antrim; Paul Badura-Skoda; John Barnes; Bentley Pianos; Dr A.Berner, Preussischer Kultur Besitz, Berlin; Malcolm Binns; Donald Boalch; Bösendorfer Pianos; Mme Bran-Ricci, Conservatoire de Musique, Paris; the late Sir Benjamin Britten; Miss Broadwood; the late Capt. Evelyn Broadwood; Stuart Broadwood; Carolino Augustum Museum, Salzburg; Sam Carter, Slade School of Art; the late Comtesse de Chambure; A.Chappell; Shura Cherkasky; Chickering Pianos; Christie's; Dr Clemencic; the Hon. Alex Cobb; Mrs Margaret Cranmer; B.Dahl; Joan Davis; Decca Records; Deutsches Museum, Munich; Dolmetsch's; the late Alfred Deller; Maria Donska; Huguette Dreyfuss; the late Spencer Dykes; Ruth Dyson; Early Keyboard Instruments; Dr Ewerhardt; Fenton House Trustees; William Foster; Dr Gaiser, National Museum, Berne; Dr Garlick; J.B. Gledhill; Dr von Gleich, Gemeente Museum, The Hague; Messrs Goble; Robin Golding; Hugh Gough; the late Thomas Gough; The Gramophone Exchange; Nigel Grimwood; Dr Rosamond Harding; the Earl of Harewood; Harrods; the Haydn Museum, Eisenstadt; the late Dora Head; the Rt Hon. Edward Heath; M. de Hen, Conservatoire de Musique, Brussels; Sir Philip Hendy, National Gallery; Doris Hibbert; Martin Hill; Historiska Museet, Gothenburg; Andreas Hofer; Christopher Hogwood; the late Mrs Ionides; Geraint Jones; Derek Keel; the late Frederick Keel; Kemble Pianos; David Kent; W.Legge; the late John Levy; the Museum of London; Arthur Lucas, National Gallery; Ernest Lush; Moura Lympany; Frederick Lysle; the Hon. Hector Macdonnell; George Malcolm; Emily Marshall; Sir Robert Mayer; the Lady Mazarene and Ferrard; T.A.H.Medlicott; Dr J. van der Meer, Germanisches Nationalmuseum, Nuremberg; Yehudi Menuhin; J. Morley, Brighton Pavilion; John Morley; J.S. Morley; Michi Murayama, Osaka Festival Society; Dr Neff; Prof. Fritz Neumeyer; Dr Neupert; the late O.L.Osborne; the late John Pauer; Sir Peter Pears; Mary Potter; Mary Potts; Prof. R.Radcliffe; K.Rindlisbacher; M.Robin; D.G. Rosetti; Dr Roth; Rushworth and Dreaper; the late the Hon. V.Sackville-West; Dr Keisei

Sakka; Dr Sasse, Händel Haus, Halle; Dr Schmidt-Georg, Beethoven Haus, Bonn; Sir Geoffrey Shackerly; Dr Shurich, Trustee of Mozart's Geburtshaus, Salzburg; Dr Robert Simpson; Reresby Sitwell; Smithsonian Institution; Sotheby's; Fritz Spiegl; John Steinway; Madeau Stewart; David Style; Michael Thomas; J. Thompson; K. Thornton, Victoria and Albert Museum; the late John Ticehurst; Colin Tilney; the late Henry Tull; Dr Verel; H. Vere Pilkington; Peter Wadland; Raymond Ware; Roger Warner; Dr Wegerer, Kunsthistorisches Museum, Vienna; Graham Wells; Malcolm Williamson, Master of the Queen's Music; Sir Hugh Wontner; Yale University; York Museum; Dr Zair; the late Dr Zeraschi, the Heyer Collection, Leipzig.

I am specially grateful to Sir Geoffrey Shackerly for his beautiful colour photographs of the pianos, and lastly my most profound thanks to Tony Miall who made the whole thing possible.